Swimming the River

by
Becky Banasiak Code

©2021 Becky Banasiak Code

A3D Impressions

Tucson / Minneapolis

A3D Impressions™

A Division of Awareness3D, LLC
P.O. Box 57415
Tucson, AZ 85735
www.a3dimpressions.com

© 2021 Becky Banasiak Code

All rights reserved, including the right to reproduce this book or portions thereof in any form whatsoever without permission. Contact A3D Impressions Rights & Permission,
P.O. Box 57415, Tucson, AZ 85732.

Publisher's Cataloging-in-Publication data

Names: Code, Becky Banasiak, author.
Title: Swimming the river: inspirational shorts, insights, and glimpses of grace / Becky Banasiak Code.
Description: Tucson, AZ; Minneapolis, MN: A3D Impressions, 2021.
Identifiers: LCCN: 2021906899 | ISBN: 978-1-7344724-6-2 (paperback) | 978-1-7344724-7-9 (ebook)
Subjects: LCSH Code, Becky Banasiak. | Self-actualization (Psychology) | BISAC BIOGRAPHY & AUTOBIOGRAPHY / Personal Memoirs | BIOGRAPHY & AUTOBIOGRAPHY / LGBTQ+ | SELF-HELP / Personal Growth / General
Classification: LCC BJ1597 .C63 2021 | DDC 158.1--dc23

First A3D Impressions Edition May 2021

DEDICATION

For MB whose loving support constantly urges me to follow my heart and without whom this book would not have been possible.

> Becky Banasiak Code 7/19/20
> *Swimming the River*

ACKNOWLEDGMENTS

To the Inner Journeys writing group at the Athens, OH Quaker Meeting, I am deeply indebted to your patience, counsel, and wisdom in providing suggestions to the first drafts of many of these essays. I am especially thankful for your compassion and support during my times of struggle.

I am truly grateful to Kari Gunter-Seymour for her heartfelt encouragement in finding my voice and to her Women of Appalachia Speak Program for providing the venues and forums at which I was able to read many of these pieces.

I thank the various instructors and professors of English, Sociology, Women's Studies, and Political Science for allowing me to sit in on their classes and gain new perspectives and ways of understanding the world. I appreciate your feedback in helping me better organize my thoughts and presenting my ideas more clearly onto paper. I hope I didn't add too much to your workload.

My deep appreciation goes to my friends and editors at A3D Impressions, Rick Wamer and Dina Delaney, for their careful reading of this manuscript, their expert advice, and uplifting thoughts and words. This book could not have been published without you.

PERMISSIONS

Modified versions of the following pieces have appeared in these publications and are reprinted with permission:

Friendly Woman: "Desert Eyes"

Moondance: Celebrating Creative Women (online at www.moondance.org/2005/fall05/inspirations): "Feathers, Cages, and the Chicken-hearted"

Notre Dame Magazine: "Who Do You Want on Your Deathbed" (originally appeared as "Your Place or Mine?") and in a book entitled, Family: a 25th Anniversary Collection, "The Ones that Got Away" (originally appeared as "Fishing for Love"), "On Porches" (originally appeared as "The Parade at My Porch")

Sinister Wisdom: "The Fine Print", "Georgia O'Keeffe: Releasing the Spirit"

Weird Sisters West: "Anatomy of Delusions", "Fess Up, Home-ophobes" (originally appeared as "Confessions of a Home-ophobe"), "Black Cohosh Blues", "Deeply Rooted", "A Look at My Hands", "Night Deposit", "Pockets", "Senseless", "Stand Up, Sit Down, Fight, Fight, Fight" (originally appeared as "Pee All That You Can Pee"), "Unfaithful", "The Clean Plate Club" (originally appeared as "Baby Steps"), "This Fall of Tears", "The Unspeakable Grinch" (originally appeared as "Visions of Sugar Plums")

Women in the Outdoors: "Hunting for Dad"

Becky Banasiak Code 7/19/20

Swimming the River

CONTENTS

BALLS AND CHAINS 5
   Feathers, Cages, and the Chicken-Hearted 7
   The Fine Print 13
   Anatomy of Delusions 19
   'Fess Up, Home-ophobes! 23
   Who Do You Want on Your Deathbed? 27
   Stand Up, Sit Down, Fight, Fight, Fight 32
   Black Cohosh Blues 36

OFF THE GRID 37
   Cotton Kills 39
   Deeply Rooted 46
   Desert Eyes 50
   A Look at My Hands 57
   Night Deposit 63
   Pockets 64
   Senseless 69
   Unfaithful 70

GOOD GRIEF 75
   The Clean Plate Club 77
   This Fall of Tears 82
   Hunting for Dad 87
   The Ones That Got Away 88
   The Unspeakable Grinch 93

SPIRIT ON THE EDGE 97
   The Ties that Grind 99
   Georgia O'Keeffe: Releasing the Spirit 108
   On Porches 113
   Resurrecting Christmas 117

About the Author 123

Everybody has their own river. You must swim in your own river. If you don't swim in your own river, you will drown.
— Orestes Valdez, Cuban shamanic healer

4

BALLS AND CHAINS

Feathers, Cages, and the Chicken-Hearted

A few years ago, my partner was struggling to decide whether to resign her faculty position in order to take a whole new direction in her life. It wasn't just giving up tenure and a good income with benefits; it was also letting go of a professional identity she had invested in for over twenty years. What made her decision even more terrifying was that I was teaching only part-time, having quit my job some time before in order to write.

During this spell of tossing and turning, we were awakened every morning for several weeks by a fat robin banging his head on the dark glass of our French doors leading out to our deck. No matter how often we'd chase him away and Windex off the tufts of feathers and bird poop streaking down the window, he'd zoom back to the railing, puff out his chest, and crash again and again into his "rival" reflected in the glass.

It was clear to me that my partner needed to leave this job that had been a constant head-butting with her departmental administrators ever since she started. It was quite apparent that she needed to finally follow the nudgings of her heart into work that more directly fed her soul. And the daily bangings of this hardheaded robin merely confirmed my convictions.

It made me wish I had been graced with such a clue when I was a brand-spanking-new assistant professor, still shiny from the mint. I had been awarded a large five-year NIH grant to study nerve connections between the brain and the inner ear.

"This is so great!" my colleagues bubbled as word spread. "Aren't you excited!"

I could only smile weakly, pop more Tums into my mouth and hide in the bathroom to cry.

All those years as a graduate student and a postdoc, all that time, energy, and ego gathering preliminary data, writing the grant proposal, and submitting it to funding agencies—why did it now feel as if a piano had suddenly fallen on my chest? Perhaps I'd be happier teaching 100 percent of my time instead of 20 percent.

"Those who can't do research, teach," my mentors had drilled into me, mentors who had written me glowing letters of recommendation. What could I say to them? Sorry, I'd rather be a mere instructor, the low man on the academic totem pole? How could I refuse a grant award? How could I refuse what every other young scientist would give one of their kidneys for, what we all had been groomed for?

A grant means money to collaborate with colleagues on interesting projects, to fly to exotic places (i.e., anywhere but here) to present your data, and to hire technicians to do the lab scut work. A grant is a badge of honor, and, in my mind, a ticket to the five-bedroom house, the Armani suit, the Mercedes convertible separating the academic elites from the lab putterers, the dead wood, the research nobodies. Refusing a grant award would be research suicide.

Better to ignore the faint pippings in my heart and continue the course, feathering the tenure nest with more grants and strings of publications, shiny bits of accolades and recognition from colleagues, department chair, and college dean. Besides, it felt so good to preen in the sunny success reflected in the eyes of my mentors and advisors, to be recognized as part of the next flock of up-and-coming scientific talent. Hah!

When I first entered graduate school, I envisioned

myself as the lovable, absent-minded professor, happily working away in my lab until the wee hours of the morning, perhaps developing the next generation of Silly Putty. After several postdoctoral positions, however, those fantasies never materialized, although I heard the pride in my father's voice when he introduced his daughter, the "Dr." I puffed my chest out too.

Now this grant chained me to a research project that felt increasingly dead and as desiccated as the tissue I prepared for microscopy. Why did my colleagues seem to be having all the fun? How could they generate so much experimental data and lay so many golden scientific papers? If only I could work harder, faster, smarter. If only I could recruit more motivated graduate students. If only I had a lighter teaching load. If only, if only, if only.

🌲 🌲 🌲

I have a friend who, since the age of 4, knew that she wanted to be a scientist. When she describes her latest experiments and results, you can hear the burbling excitement in her voice, see that quick spark in her eyes. Armed with a bird-bath sized mug of coffee, she can't wait to hit the lab first thing in the morning. She attacks her work ferociously and usually is the last one to turn off the lights long after her lab minions have gone home. Even when she complains (rarely) about grant proposal deadlines, manuscripts needing revision, overbearing administrators constantly pinging on you for some report, and the endless nit-noid paperwork of lab protocols and safety procedures, it's evident that she loves and flourishes in the vexing, tedious, all-consuming environment that is modern-day laboratory research. I envied her passion, her commitment, her belief in her work and in herself.

Maybe after obtaining tenure, I could just play around with experiments until I found some biological question that excited me. I didn't. Perhaps moving to a larger university with plenty of research equipment and resources, in a bigger department surrounded by a gaggle of enthusiastic colleagues, would get me more excited by my research. It didn't.

🌲 🌲 🌲

There's a myth about success—what it looks like, the proper way to achieve it, its assumed inherent value. We're convinced we must attain it without even questioning why. In hungrily following the footsteps of those who seem to have it, we give our implied consent, our tacit agreement, to its limited terms and boundless requirements, and confirm our predecessors' choice of this path. Similarly, the praise of our achievements from those who have blazoned the trail before us affirms our decision. Subtly, imperceptibly, a complex net of confirmations and affirmations becomes interwoven between student, teacher, mentor, colleague that's hard to recognize, let alone break away from. Any strain against its resilient meshwork calls into question not only your values with their supporting perceptions of self-worth, but threatens those of anyone who is also heavily invested in belonging to this tight-knit little club.

I could articulate none of this at the time, especially not the fear of breaking out of my own researcher shell or of biting the hands that had fed me.

I received a second NIH grant. Who was I to question the judgment of a committee of scientific elders regarding the value of my research proposal? With a larger research program to administer, more experiments to perform, more papers to publish, I didn't have time to discern the finer distinctions between what feels good and what feels right.

   I popped more Tums but began finding excuses not to attract graduate students to help me with the project. I dragged myself into my lab every morning. Peering into my microscope was like looking down the barrel of a gun. I hoped my colleagues wouldn't notice my pasted-on smile and slightly strained voice when I discussed the direction of my research. I began to question if I was writing neatly packaged stories about my experimental results, whether they really existed, just to get the next scientific paper published, to get the next big grant. (Hellooo???)

   Gail Godwin wrote: "There is a great deal of energy and contentment to be gained simply by not living a lie." Where was my energy in dragging myself to my lab every day? Where was my contentment with my research as I spent much more time in libraries and bookstores, but searching for what? These questions prepped me for my fist major soul-oscopy and I had to examine how I was hanging onto the white lab coattails of my advisors, parroting their theories and hypotheses without developing a burning biological question of my own. Whenever someone asked me what I did for a living, I'd just say, "Teach." I was a research professor with nothing to profess.

🌲 🌲 🌲

Seventeen years after I earned my PhD, I shut down my research program. I was bone-tired of playing the snake-oil salesman trying to sell myself some palatable enthusiasm for my own experiments, knowing it wasn't a cure for my chronic irritability, for the low-grade food poisoning of my soul.

I began to pursue a fuzzy dream I've had ever since I was 4 (okay, 8, since honesty is part of this new package)—that of becoming a writer. That spring while my partner was in the throes of her job deliberation, I was lucky to have several essays and poems published in small journals. It made me wonder whether I could actually support both of us with my writing. Maybe I could attract some funding for fledgling writers. If only I could reach a larger audience. If only I could publish more essays. If only I could publish a book, I might have several hundred pages of hardbound proof to show my scientific colleagues, family, and friends that I haven't just been putzing around since I left research. If only, if only.

How is it that we can so easily and repeatedly ignore, dismiss, or misinterpret all those messages from the universe telling us we're on the wrong track? It's strikingly obvious when other people are banging their heads against the universe, much harder to recognize my "instinctive" grasp at the straws of success, when I'm mesmerized by reflections of what I should look like in the eyes of others. It's easy to forget how cleanly feathers in my cap can be Windexed away, how quickly I can make life messy by thinking I always have to prove myself.

Look at the lilies of the field, the birds of the air. They do not reap. They do not sow. They just bang their heads against my French doors hoping I'll finally wake up.

The Fine Print

48 hours' notice need not be served before entering this small pantry of a life you've leased from the universe. Lessons in patience and sensitivity may come disguised as family, paint, or ants. Frustration in not having enough time to write is part of the bargain to keep you hungry— daily deposit required. No satisfaction guaranteed. Terms and conditions subject to infinite change.

Sometimes when I want to write more than anything else, it seems that every obstacle in the universe gets thrown in my path, and I feel like a pinball in a never-ending bonus game. Recently it was a horde of teeny tiny ants the size and color of brown sugar grains streaming up our pantry and cupboard walls. My partner and I had to bag up all the food and pots and pans and move them to the other side of the kitchen for almost two weeks. I already hate grocery shopping, but now I had to take even more time to guess where our food was. Was it hidden within paper bag #1, bag #2 or bag #3, 4, 5 or 6? Before we found out about liquid ant traps, we (I) made the mistake of drenching the pantry with Raid, which soaked into the drywall and almost made us pass out every time we opened the door. To get rid of the Raid smell, we (I) decided to cover it over with semi-gloss paint— country white—which ended up taking two coats (more time away from my writing) and giving me a headache from working in a non-ventilated space. I should start painting in the nude; I don't know how I managed to get country white in the armpits of my favorite olive green Grand Teton National Park tee-shirt but I did, then spent hours over the next few days trying to scrub it out with Spray-N-Wash. I suspect that my partner somehow had a hand in all that, too, creeping down to the laundry room in the middle of the night to dab more country white onto my tee-shirt just to drive me crazy—and to keep me from writing—but I could never catch her in the act.

Last month, in the free time I thought I would have before teaching summer school, some family dropped in unexpectedly for a visit. After that, it was a friend visiting for a week. And it's not merely the precious time sacrificed on the altar of social obligations - there's always the white-glove housecleaning that we feel we have to do even before a plumber comes to fix a leaky faucet. We'll spend days vacuuming, dusting, polishing the furniture, washing the floors while I grind my teeth at the waste of time that could be spent writing. Family, friends, the ant invasion - how many more plagues will I have to endure before I am free at last, free at last? How long will I have to wander the desert of distractions before I can enter The Promised Land of writing?

Note: Real writing is accomplished on clean bond paper, crisp $8\text{-}1/2 \times 11$s, typed up smooth with even margins, computer-generated with page numbers in the upper right-hand corner. Real writing is published in fine journals or slick magazines with colored photographs. If it's not eventually published as a book, then it doesn't really count; it's just a hobby, a pastime, a therapeutic exercise. Even a book is not enough: it must have national distribution and be prominently displayed in the front window of Barnes and Noble. Real writing goes on cross-country book signing tours, is featured on NPR, and has a guest appearance on late-night talk shows. It receives critically acclaimed reviews in *The New Yorker*, endorsements by Oprah, and is discussed in book clubs and included on reading lists for English majors everywhere.

Good thing *I* don't have any obsessions.

🌲 🌲 🌲

I thought I had negotiated a deal in good faith when I resigned my faculty position some years ago in order to become a writer: I would give up my faux (note the fancy literary word) career as a neuroscientist in order to follow my heart. I would let go of my research program and graduate students, my associate professorship with its steady income and dental, my carpeted office with windows facing the quad, and God would provide me with everything I needed to write: at least four hours a day of unobligated, uncommitted time with my door closed, the phone off the hook, with no one around to bug me, in order to write about—oh, I don't know—how to connect with those around me perhaps.

Maybe I jinxed myself when I first resigned, praying to God that writing wouldn't turn into another high pressured, publish-or-perish, soul-sucking job that I had to drag myself to every day. I didn't figure that God would be eavesdropping. Where are HIPAA regulations when you really need them?

All these distractions often make me wonder whether I should be writing at all. Maybe I've deluded myself into thinking this is what I've really been "called" to do. After all, I fantasized that I was a scientist for almost twenty years before I gave myself permission to dabble in creative writing. Maybe I'm just hearing voices in my head and every sharp object —pens and pencils included—should be safely locked away from my reach.

If God really wanted me to write, shouldn't there be a tongue of flame over my computer? Shouldn't I be bestowed with the power to make life-giving words flow from a rock and with an abundance of time to do it gracefully instead of feeling as if I need to steal minutes here and there between grocery shopping, doctors' appointments and oil changes? And why do I feel guilty telling my partner that my errands took more time than I'd expected when I was actually writing at the public library or at the local coffee shop? It's like sneaking off for an afternoon tryst – writing is my secret lover.

You would think that as often and as early as I tear out of the house every morning, I'd remember how scary an open-ended writing day can look like: the terrifyingly white abundance of an empty page, the paralyzing endlessness of a blank computer screen with its annoying cursor constantly blinking *write something, write something*. It's like staring into an abyss and being reminded that this is what you bargained for—a whole day to write, and you'd better not waste a minute of it. So you search and search for ideas and words and keep pushing yourself until you're dangling over some vapid phrases you've jotted down, praying to be rescued by that creative spirit that was inadvertently cremated in the heat of your morning attempts to cross out items on your growing to-do list. But where is that creative spirit now? Drinking sloe gin fizzes on some beach in Bermuda. And you feel so dried up and prunish, so hanging-by-a-thread empty.

🌲 🌲 🌲

Since I quit my "real" job, I can't tell if I'm more distraught over being labeled a lesbian or a jobless slacker; a wild swinging-from-the-chandelier sexual pervert or a lazy not-able-to-hack-it bottom-dwelling slug. And I'm not so sure that they're not unrelated. On rare days when I am writing at home, my panic can gallop with nostrils flaring and pupils dilated imagining what my neighbors must think about my car still parked in our driveway at 9 a.m.: "What makes her so special? How come she doesn't have a real job?" Or a real husband, or a real marriage, or a real ...? Painting myself into the mainstream's 8-to-5 corner at least makes me appear more respectable, more like everyone else, doesn't it?

And then there's this fantasy of seeing my work in print, of having my writing publicly recognized as worthy of respect. Funny though, either way it still feels the same: always having to prove myself to the rest of the world, always never quite good enough.

Oh, I can read all the Julia Cameron and Natalie Goldberg books about how the creative spirit can't be pigeon-holed into modules of time-efficiency or mass-produced on an assembly line. I can nod my head and shout "Amen" when they point out my time-is-money mentality and my blind-sided pursuit of something that's always been right behind me if only I would turn around and open my eyes: unexpected snippets of time to write—like now, and right now, and now again—and gifts of books to remind me of such abundance. And I can even feel my heart melt into a quivering little pool when I remember that it was my partner who first shared such books with me and encouraged me to follow my heart.

I know it's a rare luxury to finally do the kind of work that feeds my soul and nurtures my spirit, but if you ask my partner, she'd probably say that my *'I've-got-writing-to-do'* makes her feel so low on my totem pole of priorities. And when that anvil finally falls on my head, when that Wile E. Coyote bomb of enlightenment explodes in my face, I really feel like such a short-sighted ass, such a perfect clone of Dilbert's boss. Yet I can't seem to quit micromanaging my life, to quit blaming something—or someone—from keeping me from the writing life I've stipulated for myself in black and white.

Perhaps one of these days I'll truly wake up to the

words of Cameron and Goldberg ringing in my ears. Maybe I'll even learn to accept—and accept unconditionally—all those unexpected, annoying non-negotiables that come streaming into my writing day trying to stretch me beyond my limited terms, conditions, and agenda.

Perhaps one of these days, but not today. Today, my inner Pavlovian bell is ringing and I'm off to the races. Sorry, Love, but today I gotta write.

Anatomy of Delusions

> *Gather out of star-dust*
> *Earth-dust,*
> *Cloud-dust,*
> *Storm-dust,*
> *And splinters of hail,*
> *One handful of dream-dust*
> *Not for sale.*
> — Langston Hughes, "Dream Dust"

Some people vacation at the beach; I've always visited colleges and universities, exploring every ivy-covered nook and crevice of a campus as if on some vaguely-defined, yet heart-thumping, treasure hunt, searching for that eternal fountain of I-don't-know-what. For me, there's something sacred and comfortingly familiar about the infinite number of stacks upon stacks of volumes in a college library that draws me to them—not unlike the thousands of stars twinkling on a dark, yet perfectly luminous night. And if you ask my friends, they would tell you, I've always been a sucker for a pretty campus.

Truth be told, during my various university interviews to land a faculty position, I usually pictured myself leisurely reading in the library and attending classes for fun rather than doing what I was hired to do.

My first faculty job was at a small liberal arts university in Texas where I taught anatomy and physiology and conducted research which examined why, after removal of sensory input to a particular part of the brain, some nerve cells die and some don't. Since nerve cells in most areas of the brain can't regenerate themselves once they die, this work could provide important information in helping patients with certain types of brain disease or trauma.

For a while, I enjoyed the technical aspects of laboratory work: meticulously dissecting brain tissue, then slicing it into very thin sections, mounting them onto slides, and staining the various nerve components with different dyes in order to examine them under a microscope—creating colorful photomicrographs pretty enough for publication in scientific journals, grant applications or in my fantasies of receiving the Nobel Prize.

Eventually, I was promoted and tenured. Academically, I had made it! Yet there was this restlessness, this hand-in-the-pocket, change-rattling kind of energy, always percolating just beneath my skin. Something about this job was not right; something about *me* in this job was not right: Some essential sensory input seemed to be vitally missing.

🌲 🌲 🌲

For all my training in paying particular attention to details, it took a long time and the suggestion of a career counselor to turn the microscope upon myself, to notice how quickly I changed the subject when asked about my research, and to critically examine some long-repressed yearnings of my heart. Ever since I was a kid pushing a fencepost-sized pencil across the page, I'd always dreamed of being a writer.

Fearful of doing anything rash or illogical, I decided to float an experimental balloon while still tethered to academic terra firma: I would take a creative writing course at night while maintaining my daytime disguise as a white-coated neuroscientist. One early spring evening after I had locked my laboratory for the day, I sat down in my first non-fiction writing course and was immediately swept away in a giddying ocean of freedom. Three or four hours of writing, of trying to get my feelings down on paper as honestly as I could would rapturously evaporate like drops of water sizzling on a hot iron.

There's nothing like utilizing a whole different part of your brain (or perhaps a different part of your soul), a part that's trying to regenerate itself after being devalued, diminished, dismissed. I began to wrap myself in rich, luscious language after decades of right-brain neglect, after years of writing technical manuscripts that conveyed data like dusty desert winds.

🌲 🌲 🌲

Science tells us that house dust is mostly the accumulation of worn out cells sloughed from one's skin. We're hardly aware of this fine coating settling on the furniture, imperceptibly, day by day, until one morning, when the light hits it just right, we notice that the color of the piece is somehow altered, the finish a little less shiny, the stain a little more dull. My decision to leave biomedical research involved no earth-shaking event, no lightning-struck revelation that caused me to sit bolt upright in bed in the middle of the night. Rather, it seemed to be composed of the gradual shedding of bits of myself—of layers of self-images—at one time seemingly vital and sustaining, but now dried up and past tense.

My academic colleagues thought I was nuts when, about a year after my first formal writing course, I resigned from my faculty position, returned my grant money, and locked the door on my laboratory for good. There was no turning back: rebuilding a biomedical research program at that stage of the game is like trying to push toothpaste back into the tube.

I gave myself some time to concentrate on creative writing just to see where it might take me. That was some years ago. Although I'm not able to support myself with my writing (and perhaps that's the whole point), I'm still having fun with it, still managing to pay the monthly bills by teaching. Perhaps Julia Cameron, Rick Jarow, and Martha Graham are onto something: they say that when you listen to your heart, when you attempt to move from a place of integrity and authenticity rather than from one of fear or panic, doors here-to-fore unimagined will eventually open for you.

🌲 🌲 🌲

Do you ever get the feeling that we're more than who we think we are at any one particular time, in any one particular place? Sometimes while I'm walking to the library or sitting in some class I'm taking just for fun, on this pretty little campus that's become part of my collection, I wonder if I'm not simply deluding myself once again—whether there aren't other handfuls of dream-dust waiting to be discovered in the innermost galaxies of my heart.

'Fess Up, Home-ophobes!

I hate staying at home. It's not that I'm claustrophobic or that I hate housecleaning or taking care of the lawn (I'm not a fanatic either) or that I dislike people who do—as long as they don't flaunt that kind of lifestyle in my face. You know. *Those* people. People who are —(dare I say the H-word and risk offending?)— people who are ... homebodies.

I am *not* a homebody, but hey, some of my best friends are—as long as they don't try to convert *me*. Some actually seem quite normal. Some even have children (although I can't help but wonder if those kids won't grow up confused as to what their proper role in life should be.)

At different times in my life, I have been "between jobs" and who hasn't experimented at some point or another? When I was that way, when my partner had a totally consuming job, it was up to me to keep the home fires burning. I really didn't mind all the dusting, vacuuming, and "tidying the bowl" as long as I could get out of the house and do some real work. You know, like reading, writing, thinking—exercises that work up a good brain sweat and produce healthy calluses on your cerebral cortex, just as God intended.

I could've done all this intellectualizing at home, of course, where there was a laptop and an Internet connection, where I'd have the whole house to myself until my partner came home from work. But there's something queer about being at home, some stomach-turning queasiness that makes me keep my distance.

Let's face it, there's something different about homebodies, those people who like and want to stay home all day while other folks are out punching the clock, working for the man. I don't know whether it's a choice or genetically hard-wired, but some of them seem to absolutely revel in all that cooking and cleaning, laundry and grocery shopping. They appear to rollick in cutting fresh flowers for the table and color-coordinating the wall hangings with the carpeting and—well, it just ain't natural, I say. They're not as stressed as normal folks. They're too creative and festive. They laugh with abandon and have a gay ol' time, but would I trust them around my kids? No, siree. They're too swinging-from-the-chandeliers free somehow—and dangerous.

So it's "banker's hours" for me, leaving the house around 9 or 9:30 a.m. for a not-in-the-neighborhood coffee shop, bookstore, or public library. I'll typically wear business-casual and carry a briefcase hoping no one notices its contents: my personal writing journal, a Rita Mae Brown novel, and the latest issue of *Good Housekeeping* (I don't look at the recipes. I just read the articles.) And I don't even think of returning until after a socially acceptable lapse of time, until everyone else is getting home from work.

Don't get me wrong. It's not that I fear turning into my mother—although, come to think of it, she is, for the most part, a full-time, flaming, out-of-the-closet homebody. But hey, look who she hangs out with. It's like some kind of cult. Most of her female friends also drank the Betty Crocker KoolAid, crossed their hearts to lift and separate, and took the Lemon Pledge to always keep the furniture polished. All I can hope for is that it's a passing fad, a phase. Maybe Mom will just grow out of it. Then again, we may have to mount an intervention and have her deprogrammed.

No matter how many times my partner tells me how much she appreciates my assuming the bulk of the household chores while she's struggling with the pressures of her new job, I feel like a square peg in a round hole, and I'm wishing to be back among my own kind with my own income, retirement benefits and dental, with a name plate on my office door that others can't help but see.

Remember Renee Zellweger's character in the movie "One True Thing"? She's a young career journalist who reluctantly leaves her job to move back home in order to take care of her dying mother and who increasingly becomes saddled with running the whole house despite the presence of her thoroughly capable, but can't be bothered, father. After tremendous initial resentment of what she considers to be a waste of her intellectual talents, she eventually comes to appreciate the hidden value in not merely caring for her mom and managing a household but taking the time to mindfully apply all those extra little touches that impart balance, harmony, and beauty to one's living space in particular—and to one's life in general. Sounds great but perhaps this is just another ploy by the Hollywood establishment to promulgate its subversive agenda.

In her book, *The Places that Scare You*, Pema Chodron, an American Buddhist nun, encourages us to just stay, stay with that terrifying, panicky feeling that comes when we're faced with our worst fears. For me, it's losing my academic identity. Our fears keep biting us in the butt and we can't just wave them away. Instead, Pema says, we need to be a gracious host and invite them in for a cup of tea, to listen to what they have to tell us about ourselves even though it might be hard to swallow: Moi? Elitist?

I don't know whether I'll ever be a whistle-while-you-housework kind of woman but lately I've been forcing myself to stay, just stay at home for longer and longer stretches of time, to not try to run away from that stomach-dropping fear of being labeled ordinary.

And sometimes, when I sit on the front porch swing, I notice that about 10 percent of the neighbors are home too. Of course, *I'm* not a homebody, but who knows? After a taste of this forbidden fruit, it just might begin to grow on me. (But, shhh! Don't tell my mother. The shock might be way too much for her.)

Who Do You Want on Your Deathbed?

When I graduated college, I believed I could have it all: successful career, marriage, family. But a rigorous academic education did not prepare me for the strained realities of a marriage in which my husband, at the time, and I both actively pursued separate careers.

We should have seen it coming, since we had established a commuter relationship even before we were married. During my last year of college, my fiancé was in the military stationed about 3,000 miles away. After graduation, we were married and I was the one in the military while my fiancé was in graduate school in a distant city. We saw each other about twice a week over a two-and-a-half-year period.

When the military next transferred me even farther away, my husband stayed to finish graduate school. Our meetings dropped to two or less weekends a month. Even when my military service was over and I entered grad school, it was in a different city than his. For thirteen years we leapfrogged like that, living together only about half of our married life due to career-related separations. Thinking that we could maintain a marriage and our relationship under such circumstances was pretty naïve, yet we put ourselves in that situation over and over. Whenever a good career opportunity arose for either of us, we'd grab it and work out the living arrangements later. "We've done this before," we thought confidently; "we know what we're letting ourselves in for."

Besides the financial strain of maintaining separate households in two states (income tax preparation was particularly challenging), there were also the long-distance phone bills and the airfare for our rendezvous. In one 18-month period, I clocked enough frequent-flyer miles to earn two round-trip plane tickets to Australia (which we never took).

Those little "honeymoon hops," however, were far from relaxing or satisfying—physically, emotionally or psychologically. I would barely arrive to visit my husband when I had to reverse gears, pack up and catch a flight back to loneliness.

Friends who chuckled, "Well, at least living apart saves on arguments," obviously never experienced a commuter marriage. No matter how many long-distance phone calls, more arguments erupt than normal: "I thought you were going to pay that bill from your checking account," or "Why can't you fly to visit me this time? What's more important, your job or our being together?"

Uncertainty about what a spouse is thinking, feeling or doing from day to day easily drifts to extremes: frantic because his scheduled phone call is overdue, imagining him seriously hurt in a car accident or lying dead in a ditch somewhere. When I finally did reach him, my relief would often fly out in frustration: "Where the hell have you been? I've been worried sick about you?" Then I'd feel foolish when I realized he was supposed to call tomorrow, not tonight.

Years of such schizophrenic living takes a toll. It became harder to convey to each other over long-distance wires what our separate daily lives were like. The fun and excitement of watching the local football team win a close one was difficult to relay. The brilliance of a shimmering summer sunset was dulled by trying to describe it to him later.

Things we had enjoyed doing together I was now doing solo, with no end in sight. Could we ever recover the lost time apart from each other? Would we regret being married, 20, 30, 40 years and having few happy memories of time shared?

It would have been simple if I'd hated my research position; it would be easy then to quit and follow my husband and his career. But, at the time, I truly enjoyed the work I was doing in the lab and the stimulating colleagues I had. So it was no big sacrifice to spend nights and weekends at work, especially since no one was waiting at home.

Work became a means of filling a void, yet the more I focused on my work, the more I developed tunnel vision, thinking that the sun rose and set on my research, my project, on me. I tended to forget that I was not single, that there was someone out there who needed me and my support, someone who needed a surprise phone call or letter to show I was thinking of him.

Eventually my career became the most important thing in the world, so much so that when I learned that my husband was to be transferred even farther than a monthly visit could remedy—and that the time and money I'd have to invest in maintaining our commuter marriage were escalating again—I took it as a personal insult. Why couldn't he give up his career and join *me*?

Since he was the major breadwinner—and always will be (research does not pay that well)—it was logical that he take the transfer and do what was necessary to advance his career. Unfortunately, he was being sent to a rural area where I would have no opportunity to continue my research. If I went with him, I'd have to find a new line of work.

At previous crossroads, I did not have as much time and effort invested in my career as I had by now. I was established in my research field and had acquired a reputation as a hard-working scientist, an "up-and-comer." What my colleagues thought of me was important not only as a matter of self-esteem but also to ensure their letters of recommendation that I would need to obtain fellowships and grants.

This was the pit I had dug for myself: if I decided to follow my husband, it would mean abandoning my research career and disappointing all my former mentors and their faith in me. Equally distressing, my decision would provide further evidence that women should not be supported in science, since they eventually follow their husbands and become housewives. My colleagues, all dedicated scientists, would not understand my "throwing it all away" to go live in the boonies with my husband. In fact, I was putting so much emphasis on what I believed my colleagues would think that I did not stop to consider what I really wanted.

The scientist in me tried to reach a logical decision. I would compile exhaustive lists of the pros and cons and debate them endlessly. Sleepless nights were punctuated by suffocating nightmares and drenching night sweats. By day, any casual bystander might fall victim to my outpourings, since I hoped by talking out my dilemma the clouds would part and I'd see the right path.

Finally, another woman scientist, sensing my psychological gymnastics, confronted me point-blank, "Who do you want on your deathbed?"

My interpretation of her questions was, "Will all the accomplishments of a successful career amount to much if you die alone because you decided that your marriage was not as important?" It was the slap across the face I needed.

From that perspective, the choice was obvious: my husband and I had been separated for too many years already for the sake of our careers. Enough was enough; nothing would be gained by proving once again that we could survive separation. It was time to try something new: a marriage in which we actually lived together. Imagine that.

We moved to a rural area in Pennsylvania, and in less than a year my husband was transferred again, this time to a place where I could resume my research career. I know that I'm very fortunate. How many other people get a second chance?

I often wondered whether the fact that I was building memories with my then husband wasn't related to a more fundamental decision: to make our marriage a higher priority than my career and to have faith in God to take care of the rest.

Stand Up, Sit Down, Fight, Fight, Fight

I don't know about you but I hate automatic flush toilets. I mean really. You're right in the middle of business when this sucking sound whooshes out of nowhere scaring you half to death. It's enough to halt you in mid-stream for life. Or you're just reaching for the Charmin when that automatic Old Faithful geysers up your backside and clothing. Shouldn't automatic flush toilets at least come equipped with two-minute warning, "Thar she blows!"? Rare is the woman—however speedy—who can rearrange and collect herself in those few nanoseconds.

Did someone actually imagine this unsolicited mandate to be an efficient water-conserving invention? Sometimes you have barely sat down when it's rushing to its Father-Knows-Best flushing, interjecting itself not just once but several times before you've even thought of reaching for the toilet paper. That's a lot of water under the bridge. Very inefficient. But then where is it when you are finally done and want it to flush? You practically have to do the Hokey-Pokey and turn yourself around in order to trip its suddenly comatose motion-detector. Every cloud has its silver lining; why can't every toilet have a silver handle?

But here's the worse thing for me: every coercive and unwanted flush reverberating under me feels like a personal assault: *What do you mean you're not done yet? What's your problem?* Before you know it, they'll be rationing the toilet paper from an automatic dispenser with some evil electric eye peering into the porcelain bowl: *"Hmmm. Is that all? Looks like only six squares' worth."* Or *"Whoa! Good job! That will take at least twelve squares."*

Consider the inherent man-made assumption of an automatic toilet. It assumes that we (women typically) don't have enough sense to be in charge of the timing of even the most basic of our own bodily functions. Someone else's unzip-flip-drip-zip standards have decreed that *everyone* should take only 1.37 minutes to tinkle in a toilet. Next thing they'll be dictating what a woman can do with her own reproductive equipment.

Who on God's green earth designed such an obtrusive universalizer? Imagine this scenario: a one-track-minded, "get 'er done" sanitary engineer with his (his? Sorry, my assumption) cesium atomic stopwatch precisely timing the bladder-voidings of subject after experimental subject. You just gotta wonder how many trials were observed in order to calculate a statistically reliable average and a significantly small enough p (probability of error) (or is it pee?). Was the Heisenberg principle (the very act of observation changes that which is observed) was that taken into account? (One would think that the ensuing nervousness on the part of the pee-er under observation would surely influence the flow of this experiment!) Or was a streaming videocamera employed to reduce observational error? And who volunteered for this experiment in social control anyway? By what criteria were they selected to perform? Incontinents need not apply ...? And how does the omission of *those* data points skew the results?

I might be going out on a limb here but I'd hazard a guess that most people want to flush when they want to flush, when they're good and ready, and not a moment before. And it made me start noticing how often we're pushed into something that doesn't feel quite right, pushed by our culture's one-size-bladder-fits-all norms: of course you should have a cell phone with texting capability. Of course you should get married. Of course you should marry someone of the opposite sex. Of course, of course, of course.

I've seen it in too many families, heard it too often on the streets: kindergarteners returning from school the very first day and little girls are cornered with, "Do you have a boyfriend yet?" For little boys, "Do you have a girlfriend yet?" No wiggle room there. And by the time they're teenagers, they'll have unconsciously inhaled image after cultural image of one man-one woman holding hands, relaxing together on that Club Med vacation beach, enjoying the mutual benefits of Viagra, that they won't even be aware of the possibility of a breeze blowing from a different direction.

How easy can it be for anyone—much less a kid—struggling with issues of sexual identity to break ranks with the dominant culture's relentless lockstep of the wedding march? And yet some folks still can't figure out why suicide attempts for gay teenagers are four times higher than that of straight kids. Four times! Unzip, flip, drip, flush.

So as I sit on the john, hoping I can finish before my personal space is yet again violated by Big Brother, I ponder the words of Carol Hanisch from 1969: the personal *is* political. And I wonder if we don't need to reclaim the power to pee on our own terms, to raise our voices to all the Public Facilities Managers across the country that half the population needs to sit or else we just might have to take a stand, to start taking matters into our own hands. Perhaps we should incite coups d'toilettes or march on the corporate headquarters of American Standard Toilet or stage sit-ins on every automatic flush toilet in every public facility across the land in order to raise awareness about this insidious culture of flushation without representation.

Women of the world unite! Stand up for the right to sit down as long as you want, to pee all that you can pee! And who knows? If enough women (and men) became aware of this gross manipulation of our pee time, of our right to choose how long we want to take without the uninvited injection of someone else's unconscious—and unconscionable—agenda, then this just might be the start of some other kind of movement.

Black Cohosh Blues

Well. There ain't no men in my menopause, baby.
They take off runnin' right outta their shoes
at the first sign of hot flashes, tear splashes,
or just a dash of anger too.
Oh! the anarchy of menarche: drenching night sweats
and that bloody roulette
of heavy, light, or just panty-liner days
keep me swirling in the thick smoky haze
of my black cohosh blues.

It's not just the soy milk on my cereal gig, nooo!
It's a regimen of Premarin, and fistfuls of
    phyto-estrogens,
St. John's Wort in the afternoon.
And it ain't no Big Easy, baby.
It's the crying jag jazz and the agony of tunes
bleeding from the deep dark underground
of my black cohosh blues.

But you, girl, swing with my mood swings.
You sit right in front and hum and sing
and stay for my whole caterwaulin' show,
my shatterin' into a jillion jagged pieces
onto the beery, teary, peanutty floor.
You gather my shells into your pocket.
You know the routine. You been there before.

You let me wail and whisper with you, woman.
So bring on the last of the menstrual show!
You brush the sawdust outta my hair
'n' reach into my soul without lettin' go.
You sway with my bayin' at cloud-muffled moons,
hugging me tight an' close
and crooning my black cohosh blues.

OFF THE GRID

OFF THE
GRID

Cotton Kills

He wasn't always called the Camping Nazi, but this one backpacking trip cemented him with that moniker, at least in my mind. So much so that, for the longest time, I even forgot his real name. He had been hired by this small town's Parks and Recreation Department to lead backpacking trips for interested adults, and his name was Rolf. He was deadly quiet and intense in a "make my day" sort of way and, day or night, he always wore these dark, wrap-around sunglasses.

One spring break, a group of us 30- and 40-year-olds signed on for one of Rolf's week-long trips to Big Bend National Park in southwest Texas, including this one young woman who had never camped before, let alone backpacked. Now, it was my understanding that these trips were supposed to be designed to introduce novices to the joys of nature and experiencing the Great Outdoors, or to teach new backpacking skills to those who had had some experience. But for some inexplicable reason, instead of showing her the ropes, Rolf seemed to take an instant disliking to this gal. Maybe because she looked the girly-girl type: blue eyes, ponytailed blonde hair, perfectly straight, Hollywood white teeth. Or perhaps her name—Jill—just oozed too much femininity for him. I don't know why. But that trip, he was always picking on her for something.

During breakfast at our first campsite, she tore the top off her instant oatmeal package.

"No! No! No!" he shouted. "Now you have two pieces of trash to deal with instead of just one."

After eating, Jill washed her utensils in a nearby stream.

"No! No! No! Don't you know you can contract

giardia from mountain streams? You need to wash with filtered water."

Of course, the catch-22 was that only *he* was allowed to operate the hand-held water filter for the group.

I could see she was close to tears (and this was just her first day), and I remembered feeling like such an incompetent on my first Rolf-whipped trip. I had by this time survived several backpacking trips with der Fuhrer. I had endured his manic control of the Parks and Rec van to the trailhead, his hours of driving without a break, guzzling Mountain Dew with one hand and coffee, strong and black, in the other. When he ran out of coffee, he would stuff handful after handful of whole coffee beans into his mouth and eat them like peanuts. When he ran out of coffee beans, he would pack a wad of chewing tobacco between his lower lip and gum, occasionally spitting into his empty Mountain Dew bottle. Did it even register with him when the speedometer hit 90? I'm positive the Red Cross refused his donated blood—only caffeine coursed through his veins.

"Look," I said pulling Jill out of Rolf's earshot. "There are a few things you need to know about Rolf. Have you ever seen what he carries in his backpack? He's got ropes, carabiners, moleskin for foot blisters, extra boot laces, a small hatchet, a WhisperLite cook stove, a cook pot, water filter, first-aid kit, extra tent stakes, to name just a few. It's as bottomless as Hermione Granger's magic handbag. He literally carries his own weight on his back and expects everyone else to do the same, even rookies. And have you seen his knife? He carries this switchblade— illegal even for the state of Texas. It is so sharp it can take your finger off without drawing blood and can cut through small trees. I've seen it.

"You've gotta understand that Rolf was a dyed-in-the-wool environmentalist even before the term was coined. I don't know how many times I've heard him say, "Pack it in, pack it out." All non-perishable trash you bring along on the trail has to be packed out somehow. And in a perfect world—the world according to Rolf—he'd have us women pack out our used toilet tissue too.

"For him, it's man vs. Nature. You can't take any chances. Even if we camp just outside the city limits, he'll insist that we hang a bear bag with all our food and toiletries high in a tree well away from our campsite. Don't even think about hiding some toothpaste or a tiny bit of hand lotion in your tent. You won't know what's worse: getting mauled by a bear or having Rolf rip through your tent in the middle of the night sniffing out your sweet-smelling contraband. Hand me that tent pole, will ya?"

After we pitched our tent, we unrolled our sleeping bags and our thin ThermaRest mattresses. Jill took a big breath and began blowing hers up when Rolf buzzed by.

"No! No! No! Do you want to get moisture and mildew on the inside? Never, *ever* blow up your ThermaRest with your breath. Unscrew the cap and allow it to fill up with air naturally."

He stomped off.

"Sorry," I said. "I didn't see him coming."

Rolf had pushed us for hours that day, hiking long and hard with full packs, and even though there wasn't a cloud in the sky, Rolf didn't take chances with the weather. He insisted we attach our rain gear to the outside of our packs for quick and easy access. Rain or shine, always wear nylon or synthetics while hiking. Never cotton because it retains water, and if it rains and you get cold, you'll stay cold. And it's hard to restore body heat once hypothermia sets in. Nylon and other synthetics wick water away better and keep you drier.

"And tonight," I told Jill, "wear polypropylene or wool next to your skin for warmth. Never cotton. Cotton kills. And don't be surprised if Rolf wants to conduct personal body checks before letting us crawl into our sleeping bags."

Once in our tent, I let Jill in on some other Rolfisms. He was obsessed with *small*: things are not folded and packed into your backpack. No, no. They are stuffed because they occupy a smaller volume when stuffed, not folded. Also, when things are folded, they tend to get creased in the same place time after time, then wear out along those same crease lines. Rolf also reveled in devising ways to decrease the amount of weight that we carried in our packs (and thus the amount of whining we did on the trail). He insisted that any food we brought be repacked into baggies. No cardboard boxes—too much weight and occupied too much space. He even went so far as to remove the cardboard cylinders from the rolls of toilet paper we carried.

That last straw got Jill to laughing so hard, she almost choked on her dental retainer (which she only wore at night—hence, her perfectly straight teeth). So she removed it from her mouth and, not having a night stand next to her sleeping bag, slipped it into a mesh pocket hanging on the inside of our tent. In fact, both of us laughed so hard most of the night that we probably kept Rolf from getting a good night's sleep. The next morning, he was more bearish than usual. He seemed to be eyeing Jill like a hawk, ready to pounce on her slightest transgression. But she had been a good listener throughout the night. She opened her instant oatmeal envelope correctly, leaving the ripped edge still attached. And she washed her spoon and bowl from the jug of filtered water, not the stream.

But I hadn't yet given her the lesson in how to properly pack a tent. While Rolf had me busy with some other assignment to break camp, Jill was trying to be helpful with folding it just so into a nice little package. And there was the rub: fold, the four-letter word in Rolf's unwritten backpacking manual.

"No! No! No!" He grabbed the tent sac from her hands, even though she had managed to get it all in there neatly folded, and, with the violent urgency of pulling a drowning kitten from a torrential flash flood, yanked the tent, yanked the tent from its bag, shaking his head the whole while.

"Stuffed, not folded! Don't you know anything?"

I looked over at Jill sitting on a log expecting her to burst into tears at any minute. But she had this peculiar little Buddha smile on her face—half amused, half patient—as if she was merely curious about what this reincarnation of Nurse Ratched from *One Flew Over the Cuckoo's Nest* was going to do next.

Once Rolf finished stuffing, not folding, our tent back into its stuff-sac and stomped away, I sat down next to Jill.

"Are you okay?"

"Yeah," she sighed. "But I haven't the heart to tell him that I left my dental retainer in the inside pocket of the tent and I need to put it in its case."

I don't know how but, to her credit, she did tell him, and he almost burst a vein in his neck, his face flaming cartoon red like Yosemite Sam's when being foiled by Bugs Bunny. He was practically apoplectic as he, yet again, ripped the now properly stuffed tent from its bag, kicked it over like some decaying carcass, and fumed off into the woods until he could get a grip. I nervously glanced in his direction, waiting for a forest fire to erupt with his smoldering anger.

And yet ... Rolf could surprise you. On a previous trip, after hiking a steep mountain trail most of the day, we settled into our campsite, took off our boots, tended to our blisters, and sat talking around the campfire. All except Rolf. He mostly paced around the edges of our flickering circle of light like some caged panther, marking his territory, securing the perimeter, still wearing his wrap-around sunglasses even though it was well beyond nightfall, checking and rechecking his gear, stuffing and re-stuffing his backpack. After a while, someone noticed that he was gone.

"Where's Rolf?"

"Maybe he went to take a whiz."

We waited. But still, no Rolf.

The wind picked up. The temperature dropped. We started getting anxious. There was even talk of forming a search party to go look for him. *Us*, look for *him*? Nah. We resumed our congenial conversation around the campfire into the night. Finally, Rolf appeared out of the shadows with a bottle of wine in hand. He had hiked five miles all the way back down the mountain to the van and then five miles back up, in the dark, to bring us a bottle of adult refreshment to drink around the campfire. Our mouths dropped open. Who was this alien inhabiting Rolf's body and would someone please bring him back? Because, despite being the type who could hole up in a cabin in Idaho somewhere for weeks holding off the FBI and the ATF with nothing more than a slingshot and his switchblade, he was the one you wanted around when you're marooned in the wilderness, the one who can catch fish with his bare hands, who knows which plants are edible, and how to make a fire with just some dried moss, a few twigs, and a flash of anger.

We opened the wine and laughed and told more stories into the night. Yet, even then, Rolf kept to the edge of our social circle. And I thought it kind of sad that he wouldn't—or couldn't—ever join in with our fun.

🌲 🌲 🌲

Needless to say, I never saw Jill on any more of Rolf's camping trips. I backpacked a few more times with him until the city's Park and Rec Department hired someone else to lead the adult trips. Richard was a gentler, take-it-as-it-comes, people-person who gave adults a little more leeway without turning a hike into the Bataan Death March. And I wondered if that wasn't a welcomed relief for Rolf as well: the end of the agony of having to herd us turtles miles along a steep dusty trail, of having to man the rear guard in case one of us keeled over and died out of sheer exhaustion. He'd be pissed, but there would be no dead bodies littering the trail during his watch. Pack 'em in; pack 'em out. I heard, however, that he continued to lead backpacking trips for youth groups where his whip-cracking discipline and stone tablet commandments were actually appreciated (especially by the parents) and beneficial to kids in need of much direction.

Occasionally around town, I'd see him flash by on his bicycle, tearing around curves at 40 miles an hour, neck and neck with his riding buddy, jubilant in his skin-tight, all-weather spandex—not cotton—biking shorts, laughing like a banshee through coffee-stained teeth, with the wind rippling through his unhelmetted hair, and the sun sparkling off his dark, bug-splattered, wrap-around sunglasses. And, for some inexplicable reason, my eyes would swell with tears and I, too, would be filled with joy.

Deeply Rooted

Lovers don't just meet somewhere
They have been inside each other all along.
— Jelaluddin Rumi

My seven-year-old nephew has wanted to be a farmer ever since I can remember. Even before he could walk, I rarely saw him playing with anything other than plastic hoes, rakes, shovels, anything that could sink into and turn over the land. In his basement, he has set up a whole plastic farm complete with barns, cows, tractors, silos, fences. His bedroom could be a display showcase for the John Deere Company. When he slips under his John Deere bedspread and in between his John Deere sheets, wearing his John Deere pajamas and baseball cap, it's hard to tell where bed ends and boy begins; except for his face, he appears to be camouflaged in John Deere.

    For the past two years, he has been learning how to drive a real tractor, bumping along with his dad during the plowing and cultivating seasons. Come a late spring evening after supper, I've seen him follow his father into the soy bean fields behind the house, bending down to crumble dirt clods with his hands and examining the first tender green shoots that have dared to break the surface. During the fall harvest, he prefers to ride the combine with his grandpa rather than go fishing at the lake. Whether his attraction to and aptitude for the farming life is biologically innate or culturally acquired seems rather irrelevant—his almost spiritual connection to the land appears to be deeply rooted in his soul.

Easter had come early that year, but winter had stayed late, and as I drove through the quiescent farmlands of northwest Ohio, I noticed the stubble of brittle corn stalks occasionally piercing through the thin veneer of snow. My passenger, my new best friend, was going to her parents' home for Easter. I would drop her off before continuing on a few more hours to spend the weekend with some of my family.

For the previous six weeks, she and I had been getting together regularly for dinner and conversation, walks after work, videos at her place or mine. I had grown increasingly comfortable with her, telling her about my life, why I had decided to resign from my faculty position at the medical school, about my dreams of becoming a writer. She had encouraged me to follow my heart, to pay attention to what I was drawn to, to allow Spirit to lead me. I had told her things I had never told anyone before, not even my husband (especially not my husband), thinking that that was just due to the special, intimate bond that many women seem to have between one another.

But there was one gnawing thing that I had refused to tell her—to tell myself—and I flopped and floundered in that conversation in the car much like a freshly caught fish on a rickety, paint-peeling dock. Yet, somehow I felt I needed to pull this slippery thing from its murky depths, to expose it to the light of day.

I reached for her hand and began to tell her about my schoolgirl crushes, not on boys (although there had been a few) but mostly on the girls in my life, starting when I was about six years old. I told her about crushes on my babysitters, grade school classmates, high school friends, college roommates and even movie starlets and TV actresses: Annette Funicello in her Mouseketeer ears, Diana Rigg from "The Avengers," Cagney but not Lacey, Hope from "Thirty-Something." I told her who all my closest friends and confidantes were at different times in my life—surprise, surprise: all women.

The more I talked, the more it became apparent, even through my tears, how strong and how early in my life my attraction to women had been. My words came tumbling out with the force of a burst dam and dragged me along with them, turning me upside down, inside out. I was no longer aware of what she might be thinking, how she would accept this revelation, how she would accept me. And after what seemed like hours, when the torrent was finally spent, I felt as if a huge boulder had been rolled off my heart. I remember thinking, "Well, I've finally said it. It's out there."

I don't think she spoke for a while, as if time and space had been suspended, as if some mysterious vacuum had been created that sucked all judgment, hers *and* mine, away from the moment. She just let that deafening silence hang between us for some time before she said simply that she understood and that it was okay. Or maybe she didn't say that at all. I really don't recall. I do remember, however, feeling as if I could finally breathe, deeply and easily, the freshening springtime air.

🌲 🌲 🌲

I often wonder how my nephew would feel if he hadn't been planted in a traditional farming community that reflects (and shapes) his aspirations and natural tendencies, if instead he was constantly bombarded by messages, no matter how well intended, that explicitly implied, "No, you don't want to be a farmer. You're better off being an accountant." I have a hard time imagining my nephew wearing a suit and tie, carrying a briefcase and commuting into a cramped little accounting office in the city.

How is it then that for most of my life, I unquestioningly submitted to the subtle, and the not so subtle, directives of a father, a husband, a boss, a Pope, about who I was supposed to be, ignoring all the signposts that pointed to true North on my inner compass?

🌲 🌲 🌲

Quite a bit of time has passed since that fateful car ride that eventually culminated in a painful divorce from my husband. My coming out to her, and to myself, felt so terrifying at the time given how much more comfortable I seem with who I am today. At times I wonder why I finally decided, after almost five decades of my life, to reveal my attraction to other women and, by implication, to her, on that particular day, in that particular spring. What kind of groundwork, what type of interwoven conditions, had been set in motion at earlier times, in other places, that allowed my slowly germinating truth to finally break the surface? What other tender vulnerabilities do I keep buried so as to avoid unearthing any more hurt and pain?

These questions often plow steadily through my mind as I make my way home to her past the valiant remains of cornfields lightly dusted with snow in the heartland of Ohio.

Desert Eyes

Several years ago, I escaped the dreary Midwestern winter for a short period of time to visit a friend who lives in the northern Arizona desert. Most mornings, I would take her dog, Barclay, for a walk as the gray flannel light yawned and rolled itself out of the horizon. My friend cautioned me to carry a walking stick, really an old axe handle she kept next to the water heater in the garage in case we stumbled upon some aggressive coyotes. Barclay led me down the driveway and onto the road past the widely spaced, adobe-walled Spanish-style homes to the edge of the housing development where the desert stretched like a cat, luxurious and indifferent, as far as the eye could see. To the south, Pinnacle Peak scratched at the soft underbelly of the sky. Farther east, Flat Top floated like the Pedernal in a Georgia O'Keeffe painting.

Every evening, I mounted the iron spiral staircase to the flat roof of my friend's home to enjoy a 360-degree view of the desert lightshow as the sun set over Black Mountain. One night, I spied several coyotes materializing from the winding arroyo separating my friend's home from her neighbor's. Oblivious to my elevated position as observa obscura, they seemed to pick their independent yet loosely connected paths deliberately, unselfconsciously through the surrounding scrub and cactus while my eyes strained to follow them in the quickening and lowering darkness. Later that night, their wild and howling lullaby drifted in on the desert breeze through the guest bedroom window that I had cracked open. I remember having smiled to myself, somehow comforted knowing they were out there, before turning out the light, and covering myself with only a thin cotton sheet.

🌲 🌲 🌲

For most of my professional life as a neuroscientist, I was involved in categorizing all manner of things: types of neurons, cellular processes, classes of receptors. Along the spectrum between "splitter" and "lumper," I was definitely a splitter extraordinaire, separating already miniscule elements into narrower and narrower categories according to some increasingly exclusive, arbitrarily created criteria. With my kryptonite-immune powers of observation, I was master of all I could see through the lens of my microscope.

I am not a native desert dweller. I was born and raised in the humid greenery of Ohio, Michigan, and Indiana. In my 40s, I took a faculty position in Texas and, in my spare time, started camping and backpacking in the western states. My hiking companions seemed to know the name of every wildflower, bird, and cactus we stumbled upon and I envied their ability to lay claim to an area in which I was woefully lacking. Somehow it seemed important, as it had for most of my life, to follow suit, to join yet another club of knowledgeable elites.

🌲 🌲 🌲

How is it that we often fail to notice the very thing in which we are immersed? To see the very essence of who we are? I was almost 48 years old when I realized I was lesbian. Tentatively coming out to a few of my gay and lesbian friends, I was amazed to discover that most of them had picked me up on their gaydar a long time ago. At first, I was angry that they had seen something in me that I couldn't, wouldn't—that they had somehow been withholding a vital piece of information from me, about me.

Why didn't someone tell me?
Would I have believed them anyway?

🌲 🌲 🌲

When a woman loves another woman, she steps off the straight and narrow into that unbounded, heterosexually defined "otherness." To some, she has picked a piece of fruit from the bottom of a meticulously stacked pile of social norms, upsetting the whole display. How dare she think that the rules don't apply to her? That unfettered spirit must be constrained, condemned to a desert of shame and guilt. The more she is marginalized, the more extreme the categorizations: she is wild, unpredictable, unstable, loco. She is wily, deceptive, and has yellow beady eyes.

🌲 🌲 🌲

Every time we come out to family and friends who are straight, we come out to ourselves anew. Each time, we risk seeing ourselves through yet another unique set of scratched and blurry lenses, pinning ourselves down under someone else's distorting magnifying glass or subjecting ourselves to their notions of tolerance: *Hey, I'm fine with gays as long as they don't come on to me, as long as they don't rub it in my face in it, as long as they don't make a public spectacle, as long as ..., as long as ..., as long as ...* Then it's just a hop, skip and a jump to accepting ourselves with similar restraint—and to loving ourselves a little less.

🌲 🌲 🌲

I deliberated long and hard about coming out to my friend who lives in the desert, someone who has known me since high school. I hesitated because, about a year prior, when I had first told her about my divorce, about the dissolution of my decades-long marriage, she had made it perfectly clear that I had done wrong. I was a sinner. In no uncertain terms. End of discussion. Her response was not what I had expected from someone who had also been divorced, who knew what it meant to be in a relationship that never felt quite right.

After that deflating conversation, I wasn't able to bring myself to contact my long-time friend for some time, to subject myself to her withering judgment. Yet, once I had finally admitted to myself that I was lesbian, I felt dishonest, deceptive in withholding the whole truth about the break-up of my marriage. Yet I desperately hoped that she would be more understanding and accepting of my divorce—accepting of me, that is—if she heard the complete story.

I was caught between a rock and a hard place. Between 110 and 120 degrees. (Oh, but it's a *dry* heat, they say.)

I so wanted her to be glad that I finally felt comfortable with who I was, that I finally found someone with whom I could risk being totally physically, emotionally, psychologically, and spiritually intimate. I so wanted her to share my joy, to celebrate my new-found expanded capacity to love, to embrace all of me unconditionally. So I took the plunge.

I told her she could ask me anything, anything at all about how I had met my partner and fallen in love with her, how I had to face telling my husband—a good man, a decent man—that I wanted a divorce after so many years of our marriage. I braced myself for many difficult questions.

She reassured me that I was still her friend, but instead of a heart-to-heart discussion, a mutual sharing of our thoughts, fears, hopes, she went on to talk about other things, efficiently dismissing this integral part of my life to the margins of her comfort zone. Ever since then, that's what she does, talks about other things, as if she's pinching her nose with one hand while trying to dispose of my stinky diaper with her other. So we get along fine as long as I don't bring it up, as long as I keep "my issue" out of her face, as long as it remains something that, thank God, *she* doesn't have to deal with, as long as ..., as long as ... as long as ...

It's hard not to curl up like some wounded armadillo protecting its soft underbelly from any further dismissive kicks however unconscious or unintentional. I'm trying not to reflexively draw that line in the sand between her and me as she struggles to re-categorize me, to redefine someone she's seen all her life as steady, smart, married. Someone too closely resembling herself perhaps. I'm trying to get her to look me straight in the eye. Most times, however, all I can do is howl at the moon for being restricted to the twilight of her conditions, her terms, at being banished to this vast and arid non-conversation.

Here I am, Spirit. I've been waiting. Help me scale this anger that separates me from my friend.

But Spirit has been silent. On vacation perhaps. Parasailing over Waikiki Beach. Drinking Mai Tais next to the pool while I've been sifting the Sahara for solutions.

Trust, trust that I'm supposed to feel disconnected,

deserted for a while, for a month, for a year, for ever. Maybe that's the lesson. Not to panic, but to grow accustomed to this yearning emptiness, to accept this thirst that's never quite quenched, to embrace this piece of grit stuck in the corner of my eye.

It's been quite some time since I put away my microscope, closed my research lab, and resigned from my faculty position. And years since I allowed myself to love another woman. And in that time it seems far less compelling for me to slap a label on anything that's unfamiliar, to shoe-horn it into my narrow experiential grid just so I can make some sense of it.

What is it about a place that makes us feel more like ourselves when we're there? Where we feel energized, vibrant, joyful? Where we don't have to strain to live up to any image—even of being true to oneself, whatever that means.

The desert is stark, honest, nothing superfluous. No advertisements manipulating my wants, needs, inadequacies, fears. No barbed wire of how I should look, act, be. The desert doesn't care who I love, how many kids I don't have, isn't impressed with money, titles. I'm out in the open, exposed, vulnerable. No hiding. No masquerading. No layers of unbreathable synthetics. I am what I am. Reduced—no, elevated— to the bare essentials. Essence. Presence. I can breathe more deeply, see more clearly, crisply, with an open heart, without judgment. My spirit can float like a hot air balloon in the high desert air. Spacious. Expansive. I feel connected to everything around me.

Several springs ago, while my friend was away at a conference, I went to her home in the desert to look after her frail 86-year old mother. One morning I slept in after a late night of reading. The desert sun was already high and hot when Barclay nudged open the guest room door. I quickly dressed, grabbed a bottle of water from the fridge and attached the leash to his collar. Out of habit, I picked up the old axe handle next to the water heater in the garage. Barclay headed down the driveway, snuffling at the gravel and pulling me along, turning left when he reached the road. We started walking past the neighbor's house but didn't get far when, there, about thirty yards ahead, in broad daylight, two, three coyotes emerged from the arroyo and padded to the middle of the blacktop. I stopped in my tracks. Barclay did the same but, surprisingly, didn't make a sound. For some time, the coyotes' clear yellow eyes bored steadily into mine as the sun beat down on all of us, as the axe handle grew increasingly ludicrous in my hand. Finally, as if somehow satisfied, as if seeing nothing they hadn't seen before, they smiled that little coyote smile, turned off the unlined blacktop and disappeared among the prickly pear, sagebrush, and sand.

A Look at My Hands

I have always been reluctant to look at my naked body. When I take a shower, I quickly towel off in a detached, clinical sort of way and I avoid looking into the mirror. It's not what you think; I'm not overweight. I've been thin all my life. I've been told I'm lucky being able to eat whatever I want when I want. And I'm not ugly. I've always thought I've had an attractive face in some quirky way that I've found difficult to describe. No, it's a different kind of reluctance. Most of the time when I look in the mirror, I lean in close so that I can only see my face. I search deep into my eyes, hoping that, maybe this time, they'll yield some comforting answer as to who I really am. The rest of my body escapes reflection in the mirror so that I, too, can avoid reflecting on certain parts of my body: my breasts, my butt, my tummy and the mound below; those body parts that don't fit the image of who I always thought I was.

🌲 🌲 🌲

I can't remember a time when I haven't been self-conscious, even a little, of my hands. I was such a nail-biter when I was a kid, unconsciously forming these tiny little Himalayan peaks at the end of every one of my digits. I would only make it worse by trying to even up one jagged nail with its neighbor. Of course, I never could. Before I knew it, I barely had any nails left to get a tooth under. My folks didn't help matters either. They would usually point out my ragged nails to my aunts, uncles and grandparents in some misguided attempt to humiliate me into quitting. I was embarrassed all right, but I couldn't stop myself. I'd just stuff my hands into my pockets.

To this day, I don't buy a pair of pants without deep enough pockets into which I can bury my hands up to my elbows.

I didn't quit biting my nails until right before I got married. I was 21. About a month before the wedding, Mom reminded me that one of the traditional wedding photographs would be of my left hand along with my husband's, wearing our new wedding bands. "You want them to look nice for your wedding, don't you?" Knowing my nails would be exposed for all the world to see and hoping to avoid future embarrassment (hers or mine, it doesn't matter which), I quit biting them, cold-turkey. In retrospect, it seemed rather easy to stop. Shame can be a powerful motivator. Still my nails remained shorter than most women's.

In grade school, I played basketball, volleyball, dodgeball and tumbling and went fishing with my dad or grandpa. In high school, I added tennis to these; in college, I played basketball, field hockey, softball, and golf and began running in between sports to keep in shape. When I played the guitar in high school and college, I had to keep my fingernails on my left hand trimmed in order to press the strings down over the frets. Long nails just didn't work for me and having reasons for keeping them short made this less of an issue for me then. Yet the image of the ideal woman I'd see in advertisements always had these long, perfectly shaped, impeccably polished fingernails, the redder the better, like ten little merit badges earned and displayed as proof of hard-won admission into some exclusive club to which, on some inexplicable level, I knew I'd never belong. Why even bother?

My fingernails have always been soft. Even when I wasn't breaking them while playing sports, they would always have some little crack in them that would get snagged on my clothes and tear away a little more. In an attempt to strengthen my nails, my mom tried to get me to wear clear nail polish and to eat lots of Jello. Nothing seemed to work. So you'll rarely find me without a set of fingernail clippers in my pants pocket. I'm constantly filing my nails down, looking out for those rough edges, trimming them before they break.

The moon, an eternal symbol of feminine beauty and charm, graces the bases of most women's fingernails. Alluring in its half-moon phase, it is, perhaps, suggestive of some hidden mystique. Except for my thumbs, practical and functional, I have no white half-moon rising from the base of my fingernails even though I push the skin back from the nail bed with a towel every time I wash my hands in accordance with my mother's instructions: "Your cuticles are easier to push back when they're soft and supple." No matter how soft and supple my cuticles are, I can't seem to push them back far enough. My half-moons remain obstinately elusive, obscured by a ragged pink cloud of cracked skin, if there at all.

🌲 🌲 🌲

As a graduate student and a post-doctoral fellow, I worked in biomedical research labs where my hands were constantly exposed to chemicals, biological reagents, and solvents that kept my skin raw and cracked, my nails dry and brittle. The base of my right thumb bears a scar that smiles up at me from the time I banged into the business edge of an ultra-sharp microtome blade while cutting 30-micron thick sections of tissue for an experiment. The far joint of the same thumb has a diagonal scar across it from a rusty scalpel blade that I was attempting to remove from its handle after a routine surgical procedure. At the base of that thumb are two humps of smooth scar tissue, reminders of the wounds produced by a disgruntled pussy cat as he sunk his fangs deep into my wrist, nearly severing the tendon to my thumb. My right-hand pays the price for being out there.

When I was still married, I'd always hold a glass of wine in my left hand at social gatherings so I could show off my golden wedding band, proud that I was worthy of some man's love. Even now I usually proffer my left hand to the public eye because it has the nicer looking nails and smoother fingers. Yet when I catch someone looking at my left ring finger with a glance that (I think) seems to ask why a woman my age isn't wearing a wedding ring, I inwardly cringe and try to resist the urge to stuff my hand into my pocket.

When we became engaged, I told my fiancé that I didn't want an engagement ring. It seemed to me that a diamond ring would always be getting in the way or catching on some piece of clothing and breaking off. Perhaps I thought I might lose it when I removed it to play sports or that it would be hard to pull latex gloves over when I worked with chemicals in the lab. Maybe I just had trouble imagining a diamond ring on my finger, thinking that a rock would look out of place on my not quite feminine-looking hand. For whatever reason, I didn't feel "right" wearing a diamond ring. Instead, I suggested we use the money to buy a couch or something else that we needed for the house. I think we settled on some drapes to cover the windows.

🌲 🌲 🌲

Perhaps if I had paid more attention earlier in my life, I would have realized that my hands, constantly exposed for all the world to see, have always been true to themselves. With their short unpolished nails and hidden half-moons, they have never tried, even unconsciously, to be something they weren't. Perhaps if I had paid more attention to my hands, I would have realized sooner that the rest of me could no longer be something it wasn't either: a biomedical researcher, a wife, a heterosexual.

But it was only after I met MB, a woman who (I only much later found out) immediately sensed my inner struggle, that I permitted myself to notice how my hands were always looking for an opportunity to hold hers; how they wrapped ever more tightly around her shoulders each time we met or said goodbye. And then I found myself falling in love with her, found that I couldn't stop myself from falling in love with her no matter how hard I tried. And found that I'd have to leave that decent man I had been married to all those years.

I'm still trying to come to terms with all that, to accept that the love I have for MB, now my partner, feels so good and integral to my nature in spite of what this culture tries to tell me, that the sensation of her body pressed next to mine feels better than sinking into my grandmother's warm feather comforter on a cold Christmas Eve night with presents waiting to be opened in the morning.

MB tells me she loves the look of my hands and that is something new for me. Rarely, if ever, has anyone told me that before, not my mother, not my husband, not even close friends I've had since I was a kid. For months, after I came to live with her, I continued to wear my wedding ring until my divorce was officially finalized, perhaps in some vain attempt to cling to (what I perceived as) the safety and security of heterosexual life. It's hard to imagine that that didn't hurt her or at least raise some doubts in her mind about my commitment to her. Yet she frequently told me how good a gold band looked against my skin coloring, that there's something about the roundness of my fingertips she thinks is beautiful. She says she can picture my hands, strong yet graceful, gripping a golf club, a tennis racket, although she's never watched me play. She says they have a lot of character and that makes me feel good.

My partner also tells me, often, that I'm a beautiful woman, although I, just as often, suggest that she may need her eyes examined. But as I was holding her in my arms one day, I caught a glimpse in the mirror, and I was startled to recognize that those were *my* hands that were caressing her shoulders and rubbing the curve of her back. Maybe my hands are just a start. Perhaps, bit by bit, body part by body part, I'll be able, one day, to look in the mirror and acknowledge this entire female body as mine and to accept the whole of me for who I have always been.

Night Deposit

She tries not to wake him
as she creeps down the stairs,
cracks open the door into electric night air,
urging the dog on its leash.
Her usual phone booth at the end of a street
of seemingly satisfying lives.

Please deposit a dollar ninety-five.
The clank of twenty-seven years flies
down the unforgiving slot.
A pause... She holds her breath.
Then the ring rifling like a shot
along the wires, piercing her heart,
she prays, perspires:
C'mon, c'mon...

Finally, from the other end of the line,
as if floating from the moon's darkest side:
the voice   the laugh   the promise

She swoons
as she cradles them oh so fiercely
against her ear,
between her thighs,
until the dog drags her home
in the dawn's naked light
and into the aching desert days to come,
until some other chance,
until some other night.

Pockets

Shirted, panted, breasted, flapped,
Zippered, buttoned, Velcroed, snapped,
Cornered, pita'd, picked and pooled,
Calculating, slashed and multi-tooled.

They hide the most amazing things:
a watch, some change, a knife,
falling stars and miracles,
a pen, a dream, a life.

I love pockets; yes I do. Like Peter Pan, I am a pocket pushover: I will gladly settle for any kind of pocket that Wendy will sew onto my tunic, simply for the pleasure of having one. My days of wearing tights and flying about the room may be long gone, but I still love pockets of all kinds. I have grown quite attached to that little slit pocket usually found on a pair of blue jeans just within the top of the right-front pocket. I call it my pill pocket because I can keep my daily multi-vitamin and a baby aspirin there. Cargo-style pants whose legs unzip to transform into shorts have, below the front pockets, these additional pockets with a Velcro flap that are like dessert to me: extraneous, but oh-so-pleasurable. When I go backpacking, they provide easy access to my Swiss Army knife, my Chapstick, and my bear whistle. They fulfill a lot of my pocket dreams. But I am especially enamored of those seemingly bottomless pits in which I unconsciously bury my hands and arms practically up to the elbow during my cold morning walks.

    I have never carried a purse, never cared for a purse. I remember, as a little girl, fiercely resisting my mother's valiant attempts to get me to wear the coordinated Easter outfit: matching hat, gloves and pocketbook. Pocketbook! What a misnomer! Neither a pocket nor a book, either of which I'd readily take over a purse. A purse is an accessory, a disembodied appendage, easily left behind, a marker of my most recent path. Pockets, on the other hand are attached, a natural part of me. I don't have to think if I've left them somewhere; they are always with me. The only thinking I have to do is when I buy a pair of pants, which I do rarely, as I hate to shop. I'd much rather wait until I get "hand-me-ups" from my sisters who are younger but have a better eye for style and fashion. But often they give me slacks (note: once pants have assumed the more fashionable title of "slacks," they immediately acquire a concomitant increase in price) that are typically devoid of any type of pocket. For that slimmer, trimmer look, I suppose. Designers (typically male?) purposefully eliminate pockets from women's pants thereby thwarting someone like me from filling them up with odds and ends that might create an unsightly bulge and mar the masterpiece's perfect lines.

If pants don't have pockets, I simply don't buy them, and if they have front pockets but not a back pocket, I seriously deliberate, for I need at least three, you see: the right-front pants pocket (my right-hand man) holds my keys and my ever-ready pen. My left front-pocket contains my survival kit; it holds things I need in case of life-and-death emergency situations: breath mints, fingernail clippers, spare change, Kleenex, my to-do list. My right-back pocket is reserved for my comb. If I have the luxury of a left-back pocket (what is the rationale of having a right-back but not a left-back pocket on some ladies pants? I don't understand.), my wallet finds its home there; otherwise, it bunks with my comb in the right-back. My comb has learned to share its space; my wallet has learned to be flexible.

Every morning since I can remember, I have placed these items purposefully, determinedly in my pockets as I dress. The inappropriateness of finding my breath mints in my right-front pants pocket commingling with my keys instead of in the left-front pocket cushioned in a bed of Kleenex leaves my universe alarmingly unbalanced, if only for a few moments, like a restaurant table with one leg slightly shorter than the others. It's not just a question of hygiene; Kleenex detritus and lint balls contaminate the end-of-the-roll breath mint more than my dirty keys do. No, it's more my conviction that this is where these things are supposed to go; they are destined for a certain pocket in life.

Perhaps I'm a pocket neurotic.

In spite of this compulsion to maintain control over at least this small part of my life, I'm often surprised by things I've forgotten hidden away in my pockets. I have ruined several pieces of clothing by overlooking a stick of chewing gum (it lives in my left-front breast pocket), before tossing them into the wash. I've spent hours picking off multitudes of sorry sodden pieces of Kleenex that maintain a surprisingly tenacious death-grip on my clothes, even weeks afterwards, surviving in folds and creases of fabric. Wouldn't it have been much easier to have taken the time and carefully checked my pockets first before throwing them into the wash, to explore their inner recesses, to pull out one whole piece of Kleenex with all its clandestine snot and snoo rather than wait until later and have a bigger mess to clean up?

I sometimes wonder how the inhabitants of my pockets interact, the conversations they hold, the true nature of their pocket culture. Selfishly, I expect them to drop everything just to satisfy my needs: when I'm feeling orally unconfident, I pull out my roll of breath mints and often spy a bit of lint plastered to the end much like a jilted lover clinging in sticky desperation. I ask no questions (it's their business after all), but give them a quiet moment together—deep, personal, and private—before firmly disentangling them and plunging the breath mint into my mouth.

It's probably fitting that Kleenex should reside toward the top of my pocket. These innocents start off clean, fragrant, and smooth, but are pulled away frequently during the day, reappearing all disheveled and wrinkled, sometimes torn, soiled and even bloody, until finally they return no more. I wonder what the more solid, permanent pocket dwellers must think of such a transient and highly unorthodox way of life. Perhaps that's why they keep the Kleenex at hand's length, at the fringe, quietly leading their tenuous ephemeral lives.

Shouldn't I be more concerned about the quality of daily life inside my pockets? After all, my pockets are usually closer to me than my best friend. Am I providing the residents there a good home, all evidence of their escapes to the contrary? Have they become acclimated to my relatively constant body temperature day after day or do they long for the excitement of fire and ice? What do I know about their material preferences? Do they yearn for the soft comfort of flannel and the whispered breathiness of cotton or are they titillated by the rough, slap-me-around-a-little-bit wale of corduroy? Is the coarseness of denim too shocking after the smoothness of a few days of a nylon-rayon blend? Maybe they're bored, pressed against the all-too-familiar contours of my thigh. Do my fingers reach out—or in this case, in—to them frequently enough during the day with a quick reassuring caress to remind them that I'm thinking of them even when my out-of-pocket work keeps me busy? Or do I barbarously intrude upon their guarded privacy during my fits of nervousness and impatience as I unconsciously rattle my keys and jingle my spare change? And, at the end of the day, just when they've settled back into the security and comfort of polite pocket living, they're hauled out into the glare of public scrutiny and thrown together with my watch, earrings, and other foreigners on my dresser top. Do they look forward to these nocturnal mixers with delight or anxious trepidation? In the fatigue of my bedtime preparations, I rarely take time to inquire about the feelings of these who, for the greater part of the day, occupy a more intimate relationship to me than my partner.

🌲 🌲 🌲

We all have some deeply hidden little lint balls stuck to some secretive sweet-tasting fantasies. Mine are probably no messier than yours, yet at times, they seem the messiest simply because they are mine. So I keep them sequestered away, safely snapped, zippered, and buttoned down. Wouldn't the courageous thing, the intelligent thing, be to turn myself inside out before they become a soggier mess later on? I often contemplate this, during my daily solitary walk in the dewy morning light, hands thrust deep into my pockets, breath mints in my left, pen in my right.

Senseless

You! You intrusive love! Give me some peace!
You've come so late!
Why did you wait
until my bosom sagged, my face was creased?
When I had so much to risk, so much at stake?
I'm a wife for Chrisake,
a wife
with a balanced portfolio and an unquestioned life
that will unquestionably end
if I can't file you away
under "just a friend."
Our meandering walks and intimate talks
dissipate like splashes of water
sizzling on a hot iron.
You, you insatiable grass fire!
You sweep the steep sides of my crackling dry
    canyons
and, like a fool, I'm trying to put you out
with my hands.

Unfaithful

Ours was always a commuter marriage, loving but definitely long-distance. For over twenty years, my husband and I maintained separate households in separate states, pursuing our separate careers. During the times I lived alone, I occasionally entertained the possibility of my husband being unfaithful. "I can never trust him again," I told myself, languishing in feelings of woundedness and betrayal. We'd get a divorce. Eventually I'd get over it, but I would never re-marry. I even pictured myself happily living alone, keeping busy with my work, getting together with friends for weekend dinners or an occasional drink after work. Not unlike the same life I had while I lived apart from my husband in order to pursue my academic ambitions.

Yet I never considered the possibility that *I* would be the unfaithful one. My "friendship" with a certain female friend felt so comfortable, so sweet, nothing like the sordid movie images of passionate afternoon trysts in some seedy motel. No, this was slow walks along a meandering river, discussing the search for one's true life calling, about following one's heart, and my dreams of being a writer. This was listening together to Pema Chodron's tapes about embracing fear and uncertainty in everyday life. This was her reading aloud the poetry of Rumi on surrender while I lay on the couch miserably ill for months with some undiagnosable malady. This was her holding my hand time after time in the emergency room while I was hooked up to the heart monitor and an IV, helping me onto the bed pan as all my dignity escaped through the back slit of my hospital gown. This was her soothing my terror and helplessness as I couldn't eat, didn't sleep, and wasted away to almost nothing for months on end.

No, the term hadn't even occurred to me until I received an e-mail from my sister asking if I had seen the movie, "Unfaithful," starring Diane Lane and Richard Gere. Instead, my telltale subconscious read it as, "Have you *been* unfaithful?" Busted!

How could I hide my feelings for my friend when I could no longer hide them from myself? How could I avoid hurting my husband who had worked hard to make our marriage financially secure, to ensure a comfortable retirement for us? Because of me, there wouldn't be any more "us." Yet it was impossible for me to remain married. How terribly cruel to deliver this news by phone or e-mail. I knew I had to tell him face-to-face.

🌲 🌲 🌲

That summer, as my mysterious illness still lingered—sick in body, sick at heart—but recovering some of my strength, I made the 12-hour drive across several states from my place to his where he was working. On one level, I was hoping that once I saw him again, I would find I was mistaken about her and I wouldn't have to relinquish my financial security, social status, and a decent man. But as I stepped from the car onto his narrow driveway, I knew I wasn't mistaken. I kissed him on the cheek because kissing him on the lips would have seemed like such a betrayal of her now, and of myself.

He told me later that he knew something was wrong then even though I took another week to broach the subject with him. We were preparing to attend a family wedding and I didn't want to spoil that trip. Perhaps I just wanted to have one more good time together before finally letting him go.

The week before the wedding I was irritable, short

of temper. I tried to distract myself by cleaning and making his place more physically comfortable for him. Perhaps I was attempting to soften the blow I knew I had to deliver eventually. He was patient with me, knowing I had been ill and that just made me feel all the more guilty, ungrateful, and crazy that I could even be considering leaving him.

At the wedding, it was hard to converse with all his family members to whom I had grown close over the many years of our marriage. It was difficult to engage his nieces and nephews whom I had watched grow up over the years, knowing that this would probably be the last time I would see them (and, to this day, it has). It hurt so much to be around them that I'd frequently leave the banquet hall for a breath of night air. I'd walk the plank of the long wooden dock that jutted out into the estuary (not quite saltwater, not quite fresh) and gaze at the night birds hovering and swooping at unsuspecting insects in the lowering sky. Sometimes he'd come out to check on me, ask if I was cold or needed something to drink and I'd always say no before drifting off by myself again. At other times, I'd find myself immersed in intense conversations with other guests, complete strangers, about their golf game, their book club, their children, clinging to their every word like a lifeline.

On the verge of a very difficult thing we must do, when we can't delay it any longer, we often waver on that razor's edge, in that painfully sharp point of time and space before jumping off into the land of no return. That night after the reception, we were in our hotel room, ready to get some sleep before our flight home the next morning. I knew how deeply I would be hurting him in a few moments, knowing that my life, his life, our life, would be forever altered. Once my words were spoken, hanging in the air like an acrid pall of smoke from a freshly extinguished campfire, it would be impossible to take them back. I agonized on that edge, heart thumping in my chest, cold and clammy, damned if I did, damned if I didn't.

When I told him, he accused me of the very things I was struggling to reconcile within myself: of concealing passions that I myself had only recently discovered; of being dishonest when I was finally trying to be honest with him and with myself; of lying and cheating when I was finally gaining some sense of integrity by refusing to live a lie any more.

He ranted, raved, cried, cursed me for ruining a future he had spent our whole marriage building for us. For weeks afterward, he blamed me for his never being able to trust anyone again. He begged that I get some counseling, as if that could solve my "problem."

I don't know exactly when he realized he couldn't prevent water from slipping through his fingers. At some point it seemed he just let go, paid all the attorney's fees and facilitated the dissolution of our marriage as much as he could. Sometimes I wonder why he hadn't fought harder to keep me, not just that summer, but all through our marriage, every time I moved away from him believing I was taking a better academic position, accepting a more lucrative offer. Perhaps I have always been trying to leave him in order to surrender to some deeper call. Perhaps on some level he always knew he couldn't keep me.

🌲 🌲 🌲

It has been years since my divorce, but I still think of him fondly, still love him. I often wonder if there was any way I could have avoided wounding him yet still feel as if I was leading an authentic life, one in which my outsides matched my insides, without tearing my world and his apart. How can I, so practiced in the art of self-delusion, avoid embarking on another path that leads me away from who I really am, to living yet another lie? How can we ever be sure we're truly being faithful—to ourselves?

GOOD GRIEF

76

The Clean Plate Club

About three years after my divorce, a good friend and colleague of mine resigned her faculty position and was frantically moving out of her office and research lab. Now a third-year medical student, she had driven herself crazy trying to wear the professorial, research, and med student hats for the past two years. Consumed with her current clinical rotations, she was more than irritated with having to take the time to close her research program and to clean out her lab: a black hole of half-empty reagent bottles and moldy specimens encrusting the shelves of her lab fridge, a jigsaw puzzle of cabinet, door, and desk keys, and unfinished research projects abandoned by graduate students who had moved on with their own lives long ago. Sorting through fifteen years of past-tense and things she had washed her emotional hands of long ago, she agonized over whether she really needed to hang on to not-yet-published photomicrographs or old lab notebooks containing incompletely analyzed data. (We both had been graduate-schooled in the g(u)ilt-edged sacredness of experimental data, but some years prior I had discarded all my lab notebooks as I completely dismantled my own research program. I have yet to be struck down by the research gods.) Her irritation quickly escalated into "Why the hell was I ever saving all this?" and she began throwing scientific journals and reprints away wholesale, filling up trash bin after trash bin without much consideration of whether things could be re-used or recycled.

It became ugly, her I-can't–be-bothered-with-any-of-this-crap-any-more mentality, and I cringed in my friend's office watching her pitch things out willy-nilly as if they had never had any significance, any meaning, any promise for her at any time in her life before she decided to go to med school.

All her grief, all her bitterness with having to deal with so much stuff accumulating over the years, point-flashed in the body of my friend and consumed me in a fiery temple of my familiar. It shot me back three years and across six hundred miles to my husband's basement some months after our divorce. He had sent me an ultimatum to come get all the stuff I had left there when I had left him or he'd throw it all out in the trash: some second-hand furniture and household goods, boxes of books, teaching materials, and office files, a lot of my clothes, photo albums, and personal effects. Selfishly, I was angry to have to interrupt my new life with a new lover to drive back all that way to sort through it all. I was angry to have to re-enter his house where I had wounded him so badly, angry at having to unpack every second-hand pain and sort through every shabby little sorrow of our break-up, angry at God for creating me with my sexual orientation, for forcing me to examine my previously unexamined life, to choose one in which certain people still get beat up, are tied to fence posts and are left to die out on a bleak Wyoming prairie. I was angry at myself for not having had a clue long before my late forties—or rather, for stuffing all the clues I had been given back into my closet of everyone-has-sexual-fantasies whenever they'd come tumbling out. On some level, I was angry at my lover for being there for me to fall hopelessly in love with her at that time in my rather comfortable marital arrangement—one that stayed together as long as my husband and I lived apart, each pursuing our own professional careers (the bedtime story I told myself at the time)—and for letting me tell her things I'd never allowed even myself to admit, and for her saying that it was okay—that it had always been okay, that I had always been okay.

And I am still angry at my father, not long buried in the silent, unforgiving frozenness of a northern Michigan November, for making me think that it's wrong to be loving another woman and that I would've never been allowed to enter his house again or be "my daughter, the professor" who he could proudly introduce to his friends if he had known I was "like that." It's a thin line between anger and grief.

In my ex-husband's basement, all my possessions—once so highly inflated with significance—now seemed like ugly ballooning carcasses still noosed and dragging on my wrist. What was I ever hanging onto all this stuff for? A duplicitous TV, a treacherous recliner, cunning tricksters the whole lot of them, deluding me into ever thinking they could fulfill my deepest unarticulated longings.

I wanted none of it. Yet I couldn't bear to part with any of it: the big house with the sound and smell of his coffee beans grinding every morning, the newly fenced-in back yard for the chocolate lab we had always talked about getting, the familiar hassles over whose family we'd spend the holidays with. My eyes were bigger than my stomach: I wanted his friendship, but also my new relationship; to remain in his good graces, to fall asleep in my lover's arms. I don't know how many times I opened and closed the same carton over and over again, but once I started grabbing things, the more I got sucked in by the relentless quicksand of desire, and the more things I couldn't leave in his basement. Yet neither my prized possessions nor my precious illusions about having it both ways could all neatly fit under the hatch-back of my Honda Civic, and I was sobbing with paroxysms of grief, longing, and despair.

Hind-talk can be so 20-20. The most fitting what-I-should've-said usually comes to my mind days, months, years after some emotionally charged situation, and this was no exception. It was painful to envision how my ex-husband dealt with all the stuff I couldn't fit into my car, pitching out reminders of our years together, a waste that should have never happened. I longed to tell him that it wasn't a failed marriage in my book, that we had had a good life together, and that I hadn't deceived him, that I had told him about her—about me—as soon as I was able to finally admit it to myself. If I could've figured out some other way to live my life honestly, some other way to tell him I was gay and not hurt him in the process, I wish to God I could have. But I didn't—and that seemed like yet another "should" I should've been able to do.

🌲 🌲 🌲

Back in my colleague's office, I struggled to say something. I knew she knew how ugly she was behaving and how she was hating herself for that ugliness too, certain that it would always be pulsing just below the surface like some ugly blue vein that could never be bypassed, afraid it would spurt uncontrollably just when she was feeling most trapped and cornered, and wanting desperately to never feel that exposed again, but not being able to forgive herself—now or ever—for that very vulnerability, for that lack of control, and despising herself for not being able to forgive her own unforgiveness too.

As I looked into my friend's face—into a face that really wasn't so different from mine despite our age, bone structure, hairstyle, eye color—I finally got it and my heart began to shatter into a million jagged pieces on the rocks of her anguish, his anguish, my anguish. I so wanted to hug her and tell her that it would be okay, that it was okay, that she was okay, but I knew she couldn't hear it just yet—that perhaps she wouldn't be able to hear it for quite some time. For it's still not easy to forgive myself for ever wanting certain things in the first place: to dance with a husband at our wedding, to feast on the attention of family and friends, to bask in one of my father's rainy-day smiles of approval. It's still hard to forgive myself for sidestepping my gut's initial uneasiness in response to a marriage proposal, for not engaging, not honoring, my mix of feelings back then: for letting myself get lockstepped into the relentless march of wedding plans, for denying the faint tolling of the bells: something's not quite right, something's not quite right with this picture of me in white.

🌲 🌲 🌲

I wonder if it's possible to ever completely forgive ourselves. It seems there's always something we're holding back, holding onto, holding against some nameless, nebulous thing inside us, like the throbbing ache of some phantom limb that can never be soothed, a deepening emptiness that no amount of mindless hoarding can ever completely fill.

Perhaps the inability to forgive ourselves is just another form of hoarding: our transgressions piling up higher and heavier merely because we think we—and we alone—possess them. Perhaps the first step in forgiving ourselves is recognizing ourselves in someone we *can* forgive.

This Fall of Tears

It happens at this time of year, every year. Days grow shorter, mornings colder, and tears start falling from the limb of the eyelid, hanging from the stem of the nose.

A friend of mine has five children, four of whom have already left home for college or their own married lives. This fall her youngest, a daughter, the baby of the family, recently moved out of the house to start her freshman year at a not-too-distant community college. For several days afterwards, my friend cried uncontrollably, knowing that her life would never be the same, even though her daughter is less than a two-hour drive from home, even though she was coming home the very next weekend.

My tearful friend didn't find much consolation in being reminded that her daughter will always be her daughter or that she's just experiencing the empty nest syndrome. (Easy for me to say, I who have never had children.) It didn't help for other mothers to tell her, "Oh, I went through this too. You'll get over it." Rationality is no band-aid for the heart.

And it made me wonder how many times this scene was being re-enacted in homes across the country, and how often people (mostly women) feel like they have to deal single-handedly with their own grief while those around them quickly avert their eyes, focus on their own particular nut, tuck tail and scurry into their holes of jobs, hobbies, or favorite charities. It made me curious why we so often beat ourselves up for breaking down, for apologizing for having been reduced—never elevated—to tears, for transgressing that polite societal norm that forbids us from discomforting those around us, even though there are millions of us attempting to contain our tsunamic grief with a mere handful of flimsy tissues.

I myself have been crying, crying a lot, in the past several years. You'd think by now I'd have grown accustomed to this embarrassing teary-eyed woman I've become who drops in on me unexpectedly at work or who crashes my friends-only dinner party. *Who invited her?* I find it difficult to acknowledge, to accept—let alone embrace—this red-eyed, sniffling stranger who suddenly appears and is dressed in my clothes. I could give you all kinds of good reasons for my tears: loss of financial security when I quit my full-time job, loss of identity as a wife when I left my marriage, loss of youth as I go through menopause. But that just seems to reinforce the notion that tears are inherently bad. To provide some logical cause for my tears leaves unchallenged the assumption that they signify some unpredictable force that needs to be curtailed, some wild river that needs to be dam(n)ed. Oh, I could blame our misogynous Marlboro Man culture that labels tears weak and effeminate, but that does little to relieve my internalized self-policing and the accompanying shame I feel when I cry.

I've been noticing that there seems to be an unspoken hierarchy of occasions in our society at which the shedding of tears is inequitably allowed. The loss of a loved one, the loss of a home, a traumatic injury, a job (but only if you're fired, not if you resign), all register high on the socially-acceptable-tears meter, whereas the death of the family pet, hearing a piece of moving music, or sending your child off to kindergarten barely move the needle. Apparently, some tears are simply unworthy of wetting the earth.

Even for those more privileged occasions when it's deemed acceptable to cry, there is some nebulous appropriate time period for mourning that must not be exceeded: *This has gone on long enough so just pull yourself together. Get over it.* Reproaches need not be spoken. A single raised eyebrow is sufficient.

And we even lash ourselves with our own wet hankies.

Thus, tears must meet some strict standards of eligibility otherwise we might have everyone everywhere running around crying. And we couldn't have that, could we?

Laughter, on the other hand, is rarely subjected to such emotional discrimination. Can you imagine how the tone of the film, "A League of Their Own", would have been transmogrified had Tom Hanks instead yelled, "There's no *laughter* in baseball!" Not only is laughter not banned in polite society, but we want to take part in it, to share a rib-rumbling guffaw with complete strangers. But someone else's tears? We go running for higher ground like they're some flash flood, fearing we'll be swept away.

When we sweep someone else's tears under the rug with the efficient broom of "PMS" or "menopause", aren't we conveniently adding padding under our own comfort zone? Propping up our own shaky self-images as strong, capable, and clear-eyed on the backs of those we label tender-hearted, sentimental, weak? It's as if we as a society conspire to poke tears to the back of the cage with the sharp but silent "keep it together" stick. What are we so afraid of that we feel compelled to render tears invisible—much as I covered my friend's feelings with the invisibility cloak of "empty nest syndrome"?

🌲 🌲 🌲

What would this world look like if everyone cried as easily as they laughed? If we encouraged each other to put our best sad face forward? If we slapped yellow unhappy-face stickers ☹ on everything around us? Would some mega-corporation adopt it as its logo, have it copyrighted and exported globally?

Perhaps we should institute a National Right-to-Cry Day or Bring-Your-Tears-to-Work Day when everyone would not only be allowed to cry in public, but would be praised and celebrated for crying blatantly, brazenly, and in your face. Crying with an attitude, unleashing a torrent of "I don't-give-a-damn" kind of tears. No one would be permitted to check their cell phone while someone else is crying. No one would be allowed to shush anyone in a restaurant when their raging hormones unleash a flood of tears into their grilled chicken salad. And no one would be allowed to simply slink away muttering self-protective platitudes like, "It's so brave of you to cry in public."

In preparation for National Right-to-Cry Day, however, I, for one, would have to practice, practice, practice by forcing my teary-eyed self to gaze into a mirror without turning away in shame. I'd have to remove my ten-gallon hat and stop making excuses—*damn this piece of grit in my eyes!*—and just let the tears fall where they may. I'd have to admit that I couldn't always lasso the hurt, whether mine or my friend's or anyone else's, and drag it off to the nearest slaughterhouse.

But there's a lot of grief in cutting loose my Marlboro Man image, in letting it ride off into the sunset. A lot of tears in saying adios to a close amigo who's spurred me on life's trail for as long as I can remember. Because every tear shed feels like a mortal act of self-betrayal somehow, tightening the noose around the neck of my fiercely independent yet faithful companion, not knowing who or what—if anything—will be left once it falls dangling through the trap door. Who can I ever put that much trust into again? How can I ever trust *myself* again?

And I wonder if my friend would tell me, "Oh, you're just going through the "empty saddle" syndrome. You'll get over it." Who would willingly cut themselves off from the cultural herd to let go of their Marlboro Man with me?

🌲 🌲 🌲

Tears—the crack in the mortar of our communally erected, socially sustained, individualistic façade. How much collective energy do we spend trying to keep it from crumbling, this flimsy Hollywood Western movie set?

It's hard to relinquish our faded, worn-out identities; even harder to admit the violence we do to others when we maintain our façades at their expense. It's scary to consider that our "true self" might be just as fluid and transitional as tears. Perhaps it's finally their season. Perhaps it's time to just let them fall.

Albert Camus once wrote, "Live to the point of tears." Sounds like he may have been hedging a bit. C'mon, Albert. Let's really live! Rush past that point and jump off the cliff! To the freefall of tears—and beyond.

Hunting for Dad

There was a cornfield at the end of our street
where the subdivision stopped and the open land
would greet me with the sweet smell of freshly freed
    earth.
I played there after homework, after chores were
    done,
but not much in summer when I could barely run
through those green giants' swaying embrace.

But in the fall, in the fall I could finally race
along the rows of sorrowful stalks and withering
    husks,
kicking up rabbits in the cushioning dusk,
stopping to gather those overlooked ears for my dad.
He'd haul them Up North to our cottage by the lake,
and nail them to unwavering oaks
for the never-satisfied squirrels to take.

Weekends, he'd hunt with his buddies
in that field at the end of our street.
Just the guys, he'd say.
No use to plead.

One young November, in nodding light,
I walked alone to the other side
of that field and found that it ended:
a blacktop with uncontested lines
and definite shoulders.
I should have known.
As if that field would go on forever,
as if we'd go hunting together
some time, just Dad and I.

The Ones That Got Away

Late one spring when I was about seven or eight years old, I graduated from fishing on the little lake near my family's cabin in northeastern Michigan to fishing on the mighty Au Sable River about fifteen miles north. My fishing buddy was my mom's father, Dziadzia Romie. Dziadzia (pronounced Jah-jah) is the Polish word for grandfather, and his first name was Roman, but everyone called him Romie.

We set out early in the morning and drove through the Huron National Forest past Lumberman's Monument and Iargo Springs before turning north along Route 65, crossing the Au Sable below the Five Channels Dam where we'd put our boats in. Dziadzia Romie and I always fished from one rowboat while Dad and my older brother fished from another. After loading all our fishing gear, life preservers, and coolers filled with pop and baloney and ham sandwiches, Dad would fire up his 7.5 horsepower Mercury and he and my brother would motor downriver to their clandestine fishing holes, while Dziadzia and I drifted with the current until we saw what looked like to be an inviting spot.

We fished most of that morning before it started to rain, hard and cold, so Dziadzia steered us to an island where we could stay dry under some pine trees. Once the rain let up a bit, he built a fire, which I kind of marveled at, never expecting it was something any grown-up I knew could or would do. As the smoky fire sputtered and hissed to stay alive in the smothering dampness, things started to shift as if somehow a tiny crack had splintered the universe, and adventure started to seep in. I began to feel like I was Daniel Boone or Davy Crockett—two of my favorite heroes who had not only opened the heart of this country when it was young, but had also opened my exploring heart to the thrilling possibility of living in the woods, sleeping under the stars, and discovering what might be around the next bend. It wasn't just their TV depictions on Sunday night's Wonderful World of Disney that had captivated my imagination years before, but a pervading sense that I was actually a kindred spirit, a buck-skinned explorer on the inside —a belief that reverberated deep throughout my very being down to my size four Keds, and had been an integral part of my soul for as long as I could remember. And now, here we were in the wilderness, in hostile Indian territory perhaps, struggling for our very survival against the elements! Oh, where was my coonskin cap when I really needed it?

It got even better: Dziadzia scrounged up some wire mesh to put over the fire and began cooking the fish we'd caught that morning. I don't think I'd ever had food (other than marshmallows) cooked over an open fire before. The bluegill and perch tasted so fresh, so *au naturale*, so different from the frozen crackermeal-coated wedges that Mom typically fried in a pan on Lenten Fridays. I thought it was the best fish I'd ever eaten until then and, truthfully, ever since.

Afterwards, we took our time relaxing on the island, walking around just to see what was there. We had never taken this kind of break from fishing before, and everything felt so vibrant and alive. And it was amazing how different the river looked from that grounded perspective as it glided past us in its seemingly half-smiling, unhurried centeredness, as if it had always known who it was and where it was going.

Later, as night began to wrap its dusky shawl over the stooped shoulders of the day and it became too dangerous for a rowboat without running lights to be out on the river, we all returned to shore. As we unloaded the boats, Dad hoisted a teeming wire basket full of fish over his head and gloated, "Okay, who caught the most? Who caught the biggest?" My stomach began to sink as if it had sprung a leak. I didn't know it had been a contest. I didn't know I was going to be graded. And when my grandfather told him that we had pulled into an island when it started to rain, built a fire and cooked some fish, Dad raised his eyebrows and snorted, "Well, I guess we know who the *real* fishermen are." For a few brief seconds, I couldn't imagine why anyone would rather huddle under a plastic poncho for eight hours during a driving rain, bailing cold water out of the bottom of a rowboat with an empty Maxwell House coffee can in one hand and death-gripping the handle of a spin-casting rod with the other. Fishing apparently was serious business.

Dad shook his head. "I thought we came to fish," and I knew I had committed some mortal sin of omission as that prickle of shame behind my belly button itched higher and higher along my rib cage. My grandfather just shrugged his shoulders and cracked open a Stroh's, but I thought I caught the word *loser* in my dad's expression as he avoided my grandfather's eyes.

I had seen that look before. You see, my grandfather liked his beer a little too much and hanging out at pool halls a little too often. Occasionally he'd disappear for days at a time to who knows where, causing my mother and grandmother to worry sick and my dad to just shake his head. But Dziadzia was always kind to me. Before I could read, he was the one who read me stories when I climbed into his lap. He was the one who taught me how to properly hold a pool cue. And at Sunday Mass, he was the one who took the time to translate the priest's sermon from Polish into an English I could understand. He was my buddy in so many ways, but all that evaporated when I saw that look on my dad's face.

It no longer mattered that Dziadzia had been the one who had taught me how to bait a hook with a worm years before. It didn't matter how right our time on the island together had felt and how it had resonated with some deep authentic core. What mattered most was that look in my dad's eyes and my fear of not measuring up, of guilt by association. So, not caring that Dziadzia was within earshot, I stammered out the suggestion to my dad that, you know, the next time, maybe we could switch fishing buddies—you know, mix things up a little bit—but his reply struck like a muskie devouring a minnow: "Oh, no. Partners have already been set." My brother just looked at me and smirked. Tainted already.

In the ensuing years on summer holidays Up North, I continued to fish from the same boat with my grandfather albeit—I'm ashamed to say now—in a rather hang-dog, resigned sort of way. And I don't know if I was more embarrassed for him or for me—for having bailed out on him, for having bailed out on myself. Because from then on, whenever Dad would invariably challenge, "So, what's the bet?" I, like some Charlie McCarthy dummy, would hear myself mouthing someone else's wooden words and rise to take the bait. With a set jaw, I would load my fishing gear into Dziadzia's boat, then fume while he futzed with his tiny, ancient motor as Dad gunned his 7½ horses around the bend downriver and out of sight.

I can't recall ever returning to that island on which my grandfather and I had our little adventure. Even when it was raining. Even to just take a break and eat our ham and baloney sandwiches. We mostly stuck to fishing the whole day from our cramped little rowboat. I was on a mission.

And, in looking back on that eddying time in my life—a time when I was too young and too hungry to realize what I was being pulled into—I can't help but feel this snagging sense of loss, a murky kind of grief, for allowing some tender, inner fingerling to slowly start slipping through my grasp back then, flip-flopping along the weedy edges of my heart, laboring to breathe in silent, mouth-gaping gasps.

The Unspeakable Grinch

*'Tis the night before Christmas and all through the house
creeps a silent malignancy, that insidious louse.*

My partner and I are decorating the tree and hanging our stockings over the fireplace, arranging the fresh-cut pine boughs on the mantel while Dr. Seuss's *How the Grinch Stole Christmas* airs on the TV in the background. The smell of baking pumpkin bread wafts in from the kitchen and mingles with the aroma of warm mulled cider rising from our mugs. Aaahhh, the holidays.

I am looking forward to seeing my far-flung family who typically gets together only once a year: my mom, my three sibs, their spouses and kids who are scattered across the Midwest. Everyone brings a covered dish to the meal and afterward we open gifts, play board games, and recount hilarious family stories. But inevitably, my thoughts become haunted by the real Ghost of Christmas Past and I'm flown back more than a decade to a family gathering at my youngest sister's house.

Twelve years ago, I was also eagerly anticipating the first time my geographically separated family would be all together since Dad died, since my divorce, since my coming out. I was looking forward to it until I found out that I was invited as long as I didn't bring my partner. *Huh?* My brother's wife was invited; my other sister's husband was welcome but why not my partner? Why wasn't she allowed to meet my family for the first time? Because, according to my youngest sister, that was different: *my partner* was different. She wasn't family. She was unnatural, a freak, a lesbian. Hmmm ... since my partner is a lesbian, I guess that makes me one too. So, along with my partner, I didn't go to my sister's house that Christmas. I didn't join the rest of my family. I didn't reconnect with my nieces and nephews and sibs. I just moped in bed for a week—and cried for two.

And every Christmas for the past twelve years, no matter which of my sibs is hosting our family gathering, it's the same damn thing. Do we go, my partner and me? Do we not? Do I go while my partner stays at home? Because the one year everyone in my family showed up, my youngest sister refused to be in the same room with my partner, to even look at her, to acknowledge her presence. *Why?* Why did my sister invisibilize her like that? My partner hadn't done anything to deserve that kind of treatment. They had never crossed paths. They had never even spoken on the phone. *Why?* I wondered in my little Cindy-Lou Who voice. *Why Sister Claws? Why are you stealing our Christmas?* I don't understand.

The weeks before Christmas in our house are anything but silent, holy or peaceful: twelve nights not sleeping; eleven tongues a-lashing; ten tearful traumas; nine heartaches drumming... I hesitate to phone my other sister (the good one) for fear of putting her in the middle—*is she coming* (the mean one, the spoiler)? *Yes, I think so.* Then it's trying to decide what's the right thing to do—for my partner, for us, for the family. During the Yuletide, I suspect that we singlehandedly keep the manufacturers of Tums and Kleenex in business.

For the past several Christmases, my partner has taken the high road. She has chosen to stay away, to bypass the rare opportunity to get to know my other sibs and their spouses better, to forego connecting with my nieces and nephews; in essence, to not be a full-fledged member of my family so that there will be less tension at our holiday gathering, so that the rest of my family can make merry. But I wonder why none of them has yet to acknowledge her sacrifice, why no one has even said to her, "I'm so sorry this is happening to you. I'm so sorry you're being treated so badly,"—let alone do anything about it. No, they just get on with Christmas dinner and their gift exchange and ignore the pink elephant lurking in the living room.

And if I dwell on what's being allowed to happen in my family's Who-ville (*Who? Me? Homophobic?*), I get so angry and can't help but dream of stealing their holiday dafflers, their jingtinglers and fuzzles, their tubeflubers, pantoookas, and holly-Who wuzzles. But mostly, it just makes me deeply, deeply sad.

But here's the worst part—the dirty little secret I hate to admit because speaking it, saying it out loud, somehow infuses it with a flimsy, pin-prickable reality that can sound true but is full of so much hot air like a helium balloon: this silent cancer creeps over me too so that at times I wish I wasn't who I am and I wish I hadn't fallen in love with another woman. It makes me question whether it wouldn't have been easier to just stay closeted, to just stay married and continue pretending in order to keep peace within the family. At times, I catch myself blaming my partner for causing all this tension at Christmas time, for making me have to choose year after year after year between her and my family, and God how I hate being painted into *that* corner. Too often I just wish it would all go away—that she would just go away—and I hate myself for even thinking that, for erasing all those years of our loving relationship, for shrinking my heart two sizes too small. Aaahhh, homophobia: the rift that keeps on rifting.

Ask me what I want for Christmas and visions of sister-hugs dance in my head. I fantasize that my sister would somehow, somewhere meet my partner and not know that it was her. Perhaps my partner would shop in one of my sister's stores. She'd be polite and helpful, as my sister can be, giving my partner practical suggestions on what product might be best to solve her household dilemma, then smile and thank her for coming into her store. *Hurry back!* Or, my sister might have some little fender bender—nothing serious, no one hurt—and my partner, who would just happen to be driving by the scene, would stop to see if everyone was OK and would stay with my sister until the police or her husband arrived and they'd exchange phone numbers in case my sister needed a witness and after a few days she'd call my partner up and suggest they go to lunch, her treat, as thanks for stopping during the accident and they'd hit it off and find lots to talk about, lots to laugh about and maybe they'd make this a regular habit, getting together for lunch or coffee, enjoying each other's company and this would go on for months and months until one day, when it was my partner's turn to treat and they were waiting in line together to pay the bill at the cash register, my sister would just happen to notice a picture of me (*me!*) in her new friend's wallet and slowly it would dawn on her and then she'd really have some hard thinking to do.

But, in the meantime, I continue to trim the tree, throwing the tinsel on the branches in unentangleable metallic clumps while my partner arranges hers strand by delicate strand. And as I cut the wrapping paper and tape on the bows and allocate the presents for my partner and my sister to their achingly disparate piles, I sigh a little sigh and can't help but wonder ...

Maybe next Christmas. Maybe next year.

SPIRIT ON THE EDGE

The Ties that Grind

If you think that you're enlightened, try spending a day with a sibling.
—Ram Dass

You'd think I could feel a little more compassion towards my only brother since his diagnosis of cancer, his non-Hodgkin's lymphoma. But here I am, sipping my morning decaf, listening to him recount all his symptoms, all his visits to different doctors, all the inconclusive test results, all the months of frustration and uncertainty, while my skin metamorphoses into a harder and harder shell, and my heart closes down like a long series of metal gates and bars, crashing shut one after the other in swift succession much like those doors at the beginning of a *Get Smart* TV episode. I feel unmoved, distant, even resentful and angry as his stuff—albeit cancer—seems, at least in my mind, to once again take center stage to everything and everyone else around him.

I know it's partly my problem, old baggage that goes way back to when we were kids, always competing against each other, always vying for Dad's rarified attention. Dad—who quit high school to go to work, then years later got his GED after attending night school—set us up to compete against each other for the best grades in school, but like a toxic waste dump, it slowly seeped into the groundwater of everything we did. Who could get the most Halloween candy? Who could catch the most fish? Who could count the most Volkswagen Beetles on the road, whether we were on a long trip or just to and from school? Who could read the most books over summer vacation? Who could read the most pages in an hour? Who could read the most words in a minute?

When my brother and I were in the 4th and 3rd grades, respectively, Dad brought home a set of illustrated children's encyclopedias, *The Golden Treasury of Knowledge*. My brother suggested that we see who could first read all twelve volumes cover to cover. Except that—with his rules—we had to read them in order and he got to go first. Around volume six, I finally realized (sharp knife in the drawer that I was) that I could never overtake him because he was always reading the volume ahead of me. So I decided to start reading only what was interesting to me, not only reading chapters out of order, but—horror of horrors—even whole volumes out of order. When he found out, you'd have sworn that the earth tilted more than the usual 23.5 degrees from its vertical axis (volume 8, chapter 3: *The Planets and Their Rotation*). Like feeding a kid way too much chocolate way too early in life, reading *The Golden Treasury of Knowledge* set us both on that insidious path of factoid addiction. Even as adults, we can't play Scrabble, Trivial Pursuit, or any other board game together without the intellectual War of the Wor(l)ds breaking out. One-upsmanship instead of support for each other is the silently spinning, broken record of our lives.

Living and working two states apart as we do, my brother and I rarely have the opportunity to get together. And when we do, it's usually for some large family gathering when it's hard to talk one-on-one. Every year, however, he does send out his computerized Christmas letter to beaucoup friends and family, me included, and every year, like Charlie Brown hoping to finally kick the football held in place by Lucy, I get my hopes up that there'll be some personal note in there, hand-written especially for me. But instead, when I open the envelope, I get Lucied: there's just a Curriculum Vitae of all his accomplishments in the past year, like bicycling across the length of Iowa or coaching his 7th grade math team to the state championships. I want to feel happy for him, to support his endeavors, but most times, it feels like I'm being asked to paste three gold stars and a smiley face on his Christmas letter before sending it back to him.

Occasionally, he'll send me a postcard when he's vacationing in some cool or exotic place, not so much to connect, it seems, but more like, *I'm here and you're not. Neener, neener, neener.* I know because *I've* sent those kinds of postcards myself.

Even now, when my heart says I should be more supportive of my brother in the face of his cancer, I have a hard time breaking free of all this ingrained sibling rivalry. Not long ago, I sent him an essay I had written on how difficult it is to stay at home when everyone around you is going to work or school or some place more important. Ostensibly, it was in support of his having to rest at home with the chemotherapy-induced suppression of his immune system, of his not being able to finish teaching the remainder of the school year, but even then my motives were not as pure as the driven snow: *See what I've written? See what I had published? See what I can do?* Do I even feel scared for him?

In my softer moments, I imagine my brother coming to visit me from the big Windy City and me showing him my office and the lecture hall and lab where I teach. I'd walk him around campus, as if it were my own personal fiefdom, pointing out the different buildings and expounding on places of interest, burbling like a font of information to quench his fact-savoring thirst. Maybe he'd sit in on one of my classes and be impressed by a real-life walking, talking *Golden Treasury of Knowledge* (*Volume 10, Chapter 5: Anatomy and Physiology of the Human Body*) in his sister's clothing, lecturing in front of all those students. How easy to envision myself as the perfect host: gracious on my turf, my territory, the ivory temple of my familiar. Maybe I'd even bring him to the yoga class I'm taking, but I fear that that would only morph into a contest of who could chant "ohhhhmmmm" the longest during sitting meditation.

My counselor suggested that I remember a time when my brother and I shared some joyful occasion together, some lighter moments when we weren't so competitive. For weeks, I wracked my brain but, other than the power trips when we ganged up on our younger cousins and muscled them into playing a board game our way, I have no fond memories of us reaching out and touching each other. Ever. Even when Dad passed away. And that seems so sad to me.

But my mother tells this story of when my brother and I were infants sharing a bedroom, each having our own cribs. One afternoon, not long after she lay us down for our nap, she heard all this commotion coming from our room, so she came in to check on us. According to her, my brother and I were jumping up and down in our respective cribs, shaking the bars, and shrieking with laughter as we took turns throwing everything out of our cribs onto the floor. First, my brother would throw out a toy, then—monkey see, monkey do—I'd toss one. He'd throw out his stuffed teddy bear. Not to be outdone, I'd throw out my stuffed rabbit. When all the toys were gone, we started on the beds. He'd throw his pillow out; I'd throw mine. He'd eject his blanket; I'd heave mine. Sheets, even mattress covers. But, did we stop there? No. Giddy with exuberant co-conspiracy, we began ripping off our clothes. He'd throw off his pajama top; I'd toss mine. He'd tear off his pajama bottoms with the little feet attached; I'd rip off mine. Until, for our grand finale, we both wiggled out of our diapers, swung them over our heads like miniature exotic dancers, and flung them to the floor, leaving us bare naked and screaming like banshees in rebellious delight. I can picture all this as my mom describes it, but I have to take her word for it because I was too young to remember.

Soon after receiving his diagnosis of cancer, my brother made it clear that he didn't want to receive time- and energy-consuming phone calls or e-mails inquiring about his health from anyone—even from me, his next closest sibling. Instead, he set up a Caring Bridge website on which he could post periodic updates and thus let people know how he was doing. *People*—I'm just one of dozens of other *people*. In order to communicate with my brother, I have to log in and post a short response like all the other outsiders who can only reach him via his Caring Bridge website. I can understand his rationale for safeguarding his rest and privacy, but it feels like an electronic Berlin Wall all the same.

Yet, if we were never that close growing up, then why this need to feel more connected to him now? Is this just a bout of nostalgia, a wishing for *The Way We Never Were*? Or fear of my own mortality as I see him staring his in the face? You see, my brother is only 17 months older than me. Next to Mom, he is the only other person alive who has known me the longest.

But what does he *really* know about me? About my life? About my divorce? About how hard it was coming out of the closet? And how leading a more authentic life isn't always the bed of roses it's cracked up to be? Even before my brother's diagnosis of cancer, I wanted to share all this with him because I had been feeling increasingly disconnected from him even then. On my counselor's advice, I wrote my brother a long letter—sliding out onto that sapling's precarious limb, releasing a hopeful weather balloon into the thinning atmosphere between us. I told him how alienated I felt from him and how I wished for a closer connection. I waited for a reply, a reply that would warm the cockles of my heart, maybe even ignite a sparkler of delight in each other. I waited for him to ask me the deeper questions, questions about what helped me through those really rough transitions in my life, what challenges they posed, and how they might lend some insight into his. But, no, I Charlie Browned that one too. No response. Nada. Zip. Another metal gate slammed in the face of Agent 86.

I tried to put on my big-girl panties and let that go, to tell myself, *Oh, he just got busy with his teaching, with his family, drinking Starbucks with his cycling buddies after a weekend morning ride.* I pondered this on long walks. I practiced meditation. I took a workshop in Compassionate Communication. Finally, I couldn't stand it any longer. I called him and asked if he had any response to my letter, to my heart's outpourings, my feelings of disconnection. He just said, Well, *I don't feel that way.* And, just like that, with a *Men are from Mars, Women from Venus* wave of his voice, poof! I was gone, obliterated. Ever since, it's like a Country Western You Done Me Wrong song that won't quit playing in my head even in the face of his life-threatening condition.

And on those rare occasions when he does phone me, when I hope for something more solid between us, the conversation all too often molds itself into a hollow chocolate Easter bunny: a sweet shell of *how-are-yous* and *whatcha-been-doin's* surrounding the same old empty space of what he's been up to, what he's accomplished lately. I try not to slide down into that one-upsmanship mud pit and retaliate with everything I've been doing, but I'm usually knee-deep before I catch myself. Then I just grind my teeth, nod my head and *"Uh huh"* every now and then to hold up my end of the conversation.

Next comes his Joe Friday approach: rapidly firing off one info question right after another before I've even finished answering the first: *What are you teaching? How many students do you have? When is your break?* You know: *Just the facts, ma'am.* Or worse: finishing my sentences for me when I'm trying to craft a deliberate, thoughtful response. It's like a blind woman being jerked across a busy street by someone who's so preoccupied with patting themselves on the back that they're oblivious to the fact that it's not the direction she wanted to go. All the while, he's put me on speaker phone. In that cave-like echoing over the receiver, I hear him rustling around in his kitchen accomplishing some other chore, checking another item off his daily to-do list. Sometimes I just want to reach through the phone and smack him into the middle of next week, but then I remember he has cancer and that's probably not a part of his prescribed treatment plan.

Why can't he see that while he's merely putting on the sprinkles, the ice cream is melting and we're missing the best part? I think of the book, *The Best Things in Life I Learned in Kindergarten*, and wonder how I could enroll him in a remedial crash course in sharing and taking turns. Meanwhile, our words skate past each other, skimming across an all-too-smooth surface, while feelings sink deeper or remain frozen below. It's enough to make my Compassionate Communication instructor bang her head repeatedly against the blackboard.

My brain can discern the familial patterns here. My brother and I were cut from the same cloth, weaned on the same survival strategies: looking out for number one first, masking feelings with jokes and superficialities. And it wasn't all that long ago when I, too, gilded productivity over presence, accomplishment over connection. Just this morning, in fact.

    I'm not fond of this whiny, runny-nosed part of me that oozes out when it feels it's not getting enough attention. And I'm a tad resentful because for the last ten years or so, I've been dragged kicking and screaming through a grueling awakening process by my partner who makes me see how insensitive *I* can be, how all too often I unconsciously act like the sun rises and sets on my own little world, population: 1. It's upsetting to find out you're not as kind and compassionate as you thought you were, downright disturbing to have your self-image bubble burst by someone else's point of view. Ignorance is bliss. Sometimes *I* pray, *Please, oh, please God, take me back to my formerly blissful ignorant state*. Tuning in to the needs of others is way too much work. But that sounds so much like the BP oil executive whose drilling rig exploded in the Gulf of Mexico some years ago, ruining thousands of lives and livelihoods and wildlife habitats, yet who bitterly complained how he just wanted *his* life back. No. God seems to get a kick out of stretching me until I'm like the elastic waistband on a well-worn pair of Fruit-of-the-Looms. So, God, why can't you stretch my brother just a little bit too? And, preferably, in my lifetime?

    Whininess aside, I do believe that a certain amount of healing occurs when we tap into what we truly want, when we allow ourselves to voice our deepest desires to the ever-present Universe, to the almighty Force, to the ultimate One—One that has never, in my experience, put me on speaker phone. I want my brother to ask about my life, and I want to *feel* that he hears me and sees me and recognizes me (especially now that Dad is gone ...?) And I not only want him to be more thoughtful, I want him to *want* to become more thoughtful. I want my brother to rise from his unconscious insensitivity and be as excited about it as if he were Lazarus leaping out of his tomb for a hot date. But that was like my desire for George W. Bush to *want* to care about the homeless after hurricane Katrina and the unemployed and ending the war instead of just landing on an aircraft carrier—*Mission Accomplished!*

Buddhist philosophers teach that we create our own suffering by craving the unattainable. Perhaps they're right. I picture parents expecting a toddler to sit still in church and pay attention to a service conducted in a language he can't understand. Perhaps I'm expecting that of my brother. Maybe he's just not capable of the type of communication I want right now no matter how much I wish he may, I wish he might.

Sometimes it feels that my relationship with my brother is like the one I have with coffee: I love the aroma and the sound of it perking; I just can't drink it without it upsetting my stomach. Yet, as I try to settle for the instant decaf version—the Buddhist blend—it makes me wonder, is it possible for me to feel compassion for his plight without a stronger connection? Is it possible for two to tango when one is so unmoving—and the other so unmoved? I'm not sure, but these things waft through my mind like the steam rising from my mug, swirling with dreams of yet another laughingly naked, uninhibited moment with my only brother.

Georgia O'Keeffe: Releasing the Spirit

Yesterday I found myself crying in the Columbus Museum of Art as I viewed the exhibit entitled, "Georgia O'Keeffe and New Mexico: A Sense of Place." My partner and I had made a special trip to the big city in the middle of December in order to see it. She may not completely understand but she is sensitive to my inexplicably deep attraction to O'Keeffe's life and her work. This trip was her early Christmas present to me.

I was first introduced to the art of Georgia O'Keeffe in the mid-1990s when a friend sent me a postcard displaying one of O'Keeffe's famous paintings of a cow's skull entitled, "Red, White, and Blue," (1931). I had never seen it before. As an anatomist, I had studied plenty of skull bones in my career yet I was so intrigued by O'Keeffe's rendering of this image that I went to the college library for information about the artist. There I found and quickly devoured a book about O'Keeffe's life when I should have been working on experiments in my laboratory.

In the following years, I would go to bookstores and instead of browsing in the science section, I'd find myself hurrying straight for the art section to read the latest book about this remarkable spirit named O'Keeffe. At the time, I was living in Texas so one October, I drove across the state to Canyon, Texas to visit the college where she had taught art classes and to hike the trails of Palo Duro Canyon that had inspired some of her earlier work. Another time I went in search of her home in Abiquiu, New Mexico just to see where she lived, only to find that one needed to make a reservation several months in advance to take the tour. It wasn't until after I had moved to the Midwest that I was finally able to make a special trip back to Abiquiu to tour the inside of her home and studio—more than four years later.

When I first read about O'Keeffe's life, there were some similarities about our lives that struck me as especially significant: she had moved from the East to take a teaching position in Texas much as I had done; while there, she had fallen in love with the land and the seemingly limitless sky of the desert Southwest much as I had done; and she had lived apart from her husband for long periods of time just as I had during most of my married life. When I first became acquainted with O'Keeffe's work, I was struggling with my own internalized homophobia. Although O'Keeffe's sexual orientation might be debated by those who somehow consider it important, it was how passionately she seemed to live her life that, in part, gave me the courage to eventually pursue my own passions—to resign my faculty position in order to become a writer, and to fall in love with another woman—two things I had always dreamed about, but refused to consider, ever since I was a kid.

Viewing O'Keeffe's New Mexico landscapes in the Columbus art museum that day with my partner, I was overcome by a nameless emotion, unplanned, unpremeditated. It wasn't until after I had left the exhibit that I tried to explain my tears, more to myself than to my partner. It seemed that I wasn't merely caught up with the beauty of O'Keeffe's work—I had fallen in love with her paintings of New Mexico long before when I had first moved to Texas. It wasn't just longing to be back hiking in New Mexico as I had done frequently when I still lived out West. And it was not just gratitude for being in this special place on this crisp December day with a loving partner who wanted to share this experience with me.

Could this emotion be the essence of art, of that which passes between people and endures across the vast plains of time and space? We each extract our own particular meanings from our individual experiences and I'm sure that that part of the country held different meanings for O'Keeffe and me, meanings that changed for us each time we found ourselves embraced by the unembarrassed spirit of the Land of Enchantment. Her aesthetic for the New Mexico landscape may have been similar to mine—or not. But the fact that something about the land is capable of invoking a certain kind of feeling—a certain kind of energy—at all, perhaps approximates more closely the essence that endures, the thing that connects artist, subject, and viewer.

Keeping that connection alive, keeping that open channel—that willingness to experience that energy in the first place—to the land or whatever it is that inspires you, then wanting to share it with others— feeling compelled to share it with others—is perhaps what artists are all about. Yet art is, on some level, doing it for yourself, all for yourself, only for yourself. O'Keeffe said about the Pedernal, "God told me if I painted that mountain often enough, He'd give it to me."

How is it then that, as an unintended consequence long after you're dead, that work of yours (which isn't really yours, having been inspired by the beauty, the spirit, the essence of the land, its colors, shapes and shadows), can transcend time and space to invoke similar feelings in those who view it? How is that possible? It's surely not something that can be visualized at the time. It can't be framed. There is no paint-by-number, stay-within-the-lines kind of template to follow. It's a messy process of sitting down with your work, with what *draws you*—even if you think you're drawing *it*—whether it be a blue-flat-topped mountain or a giant calla lily. You don't analyze, you don't label, you don't try to be clever or come up with answers or even with a plan. You just paint, draw, sing, dance, play, write what you feel at that moment—honestly, completely, with integrity. Any thought of a possible audience for your work can ruin it.

Often I find it difficult to express in words the emotions that I feel. I don't think I'm alone in this. Perhaps O'Keeffe was no different: while viewing her paintings I had a sense of her striving to express her feelings—then and there, on that particular day in mid-December—and using paint, no less. In the sacred hush of that art museum, I could almost feel her struggle resonating within me, her grappling to get the colors, hues, and textures of the red hills down just right in the constantly changing light of the high desert air. Each painting was different yet similar in their ability to pluck me from the gallery couch and cloak me in the heart of the canyons and arroyos she loved so passionately, into the heart of her heart which is the heart of the same land full of the same limitless space, the same expansive pulsating Spirit that flows through us all. That draw, that pull which keeps me in touch with the spirit of that place, that melting of barriers between me and the rest of the universe—perhaps it was those boundaries that dissolved into tears as I viewed the O'Keeffe exhibit with my partner.

Rumi, the Sufi poet and mystic, said, "The most living thing is when the eyes of two lovers meet and in what passes between them then." In retrospect, what passed between O'Keeffe and me that afternoon, what touched my heart across the vast expanse of time and space between her painting those hills around Ghost Ranch, New Mexico and my viewing them that day in Columbus, Ohio, and across our different generational viewpoints and cultural perspectives, seemed to me to be such a living thing, such a powerful thing.

How can we capture this spirit that reaches out to us in so many ways if only we would pay attention, if only we would want to be connected, if only we would want to be so embraced? For to have any preconceived idea of what that connection even looks like, feels like, sounds like, would, a priori, foreclose on its infinitely abundant possibilities and transform it into just another empty commodity to pursue and possess. I couldn't have imagined before entering the Columbus Museum of Art that I'd be crying at the sight of O'Keeffe's paintings, many that I had seen before in books and at other exhibits in Dallas, Santa Fe, and Ft. Wayne. I couldn't have foreseen what my eyes would be open to, what my heart would be opened to, that day as I sat in the heart of that place.

Perhaps I should recognize my human inadequacies in attempting to capture a Spirit that can't be contained. Perhaps I should resist the urge to explain the unexplainable, to analyze the unanalyzable, to slap a label on the undefinable and just let those tears be, to let them be what they were. But maybe it's the same Spirit that's calling me to try, to stretch myself beyond self-imposed and socially enforced emotional borders to more accurately describe my feelings, to try to connect with other readers who might feel similarly about O'Keeffe's work, spirit, and connection to the Land of Enchantment. In the messy process of trying to capture on paper what I'm feeling, perhaps then it can be released. Perhaps then it can take wing and fly on in the limitless sky that connects us all.

On Porches

There is something uniquely soothing about sitting on a porch. The stabbing glare from far too many windshields fails to penetrate its subdued shadows. A porch's cool breath soothes the sizzling sidewalk heat and the cloying, damp-shirt citiness. The invitation is subtle—just a few wide, creaky steps beckon you to come rest. A deep wrap-around porch embraces you in awaiting arms. *Stay awhile,* it calls. *It's good of you to come.*

I love porches with a waist-high wall wide enough on which to sit. I can perch on the edge of my turf and survey the outside world without being too obvious. One of my favorite things is to sit up there, sip a glass of wine, and observe the pedestrians passing on the sidewalk or the busy traffic whizzing by on the boulevard. The porch provides some semblance of distance, just far enough away so that I'm not bothered by the street noise yet close enough to view some of life's little melodramas unfolding just beyond.

I remember a kid—three, maybe four years old—riding his tricycle on the sidewalk as his dad walked ahead. The kid, obviously tired, just stopped on the sidewalk and would go no farther. At first, the dad waited for him, exhorting him on with, "C'mon. Let's go. Let's go." But the kid wouldn't budge. The dad walked on, perhaps thinking that a child's fear of separation would motivate his son to catch up. Not a chance. More exhortations. Still nothing. Now it was a test of wills. The father stood with hands on hips in palpable frustration.

Witnessing this standoff from my porch, I tensed as the dad retraced his steps and loomed over his son. Now he's going to get it, I thought, for surely if I were a parent (which I am not), I couldn't imagine letting my kid get away with this without at least some perfunctory spank on the bottom to show him who's boss. Instead, the man stooped down, gathered his son in one arm, the trike in the other, and calmly walked home.

I don't imagine that the memory of this incident will figure as poignantly for the child as it has for me. I think of it often; it gives me pause during moments of exasperation. Who could've guessed that my porch would provide such unexpected opportunities for me —an unwitting witness—to reflect, to learn, and (I hope) to follow the father's example?

At other times, an ordinarily concealed human foible might be unveiled to me. Take the guy walking his dog. At some point, the dog is compelled to do what doggies do, and the owner is faced with the decision to either obey or ignore the local pooper-scooper laws. With a furtive peek over his shoulder, knowing he should be cleaning up after his pet but relishing the delicious possibility of being able to get away with something, he walks on, smiling to himself, confident that no one has noticed. But I from my vantage point, recessed in porch shadows—the *observer obscura*—have noticed.

I wish I could say that it didn't bother me, but I was irritated at the irresponsibility, at the sense of entitlement that certain regulations don't apply. Ah, the wrath of the self-righteous. For aren't we most upset at those venial sins which we are loathe to admit we've committed? And who am I to pass judgment? Haven't I done my share of cutting corners, thinking no one would notice?

And as I continue to watch the human parade of flaws and shortcomings march past my porch, there are other flashes of recognition: "Oh, look! There goes Laziness! And here comes Impatience!" Then I wave at them and smile, relieved that their burden is not mine alone to bear.

🌲 🌲 🌲

When I was still married, I could usually coax my husband into barbecuing out on the porch. On evenings when I especially needed the respite of our porch, I'd prepare the rest of the meal before he'd light the charcoal, then hurry outside so I wouldn't miss any of the great smells. He would add some mesquite chips to the bottom of the grill for extra flavor and would typically smoke a cigar while he barbecued.

There's something about the smell of a cigar that reassures me. My dad smoked cigars and that scent was as much a part of him as that of his Old Spice Aftershave—scents that were a mix of authority and security, unquestionable and unspoken; scents that clung to the drapes and carpeting long after he had left the room and that continue to cling to the fabric of my memories in the years since his passing.

I tried a few stogies myself in my rebellious teens (not to be confused with my rebellious twenties or my rebellious thirties), mostly in our downstairs family room watching a Notre Dame football game on TV after my Saturday chores were done. My mom thought Dad was watching the game with me because of the cigar smell, so she was quite surprised when he walked through the back door after his weekly trip to the car wash. I can't remember if they grounded me (that time), but I think my dad was more upset that I had smoked one of his cherished El Producto Coronas instead of buying my own with my hard-earned baby-sitting money.

I didn't mind spending a little cash to buy my husband a higher quality cigar. I bought them partly for his smoking pleasure but also for me, for my comfort, to create a certain ambience on our porch—perhaps to extend the certainty of my youth into the unpredictability of my future. These thoughts would sometimes waft through my mind as the aromas of cigar, barbecue, and mesquite intertwined and then blanketed me on our porch wall, front row seat, sipping my glass of wine.

Resurrecting Christmas

Call it karma. Call it poetic justice or the hand of Cindy Lou Who stealing Christmas back from the Grinch. I don't know what nudged us to take that icy two-lane road when the Indiana Tollway would've been faster and cleared of snow sooner at that December's end. But, there we were, my partner and I, licking our wounds from the trauma we had just endured at my family's Christmas gathering.

Like most modern families, ours is geographically challenged. My sibs and their kids are spread across three states and it's rare for all of us to spend the holidays together. After eight years of being a couple, my partner had not even met some of my immediate family, let alone forged any kind of common bonds with them. And they had had little chance to get to know her better.

That particular Christmas, however, was the miracle on ice: my whole family was finally going to be together. I was so looking forward to seeing everyone, retelling inside family jokes and stories, playing Euchre, and sitting down to a big meal together—all those things that help make a family a family. I closed my eyes and dreamt of the Currier and Ives Christmas that we would have that day.

We didn't.

From the moment my sister walked in, it was all too obvious that she didn't want to be there—didn't want us to be there. The look on her face was, *How dare I bring my partner to our family's—her family's—Christmas?* How dare I rub our relationship in my sister's face? For the rest of the day, she refused to acknowledge my partner or me, looking through us, past us, away from us as if we were some hideous ghosts from Christmas present and, hopefully, never to be in her Christmas future. I had hoped that my sister had forgiven me for divorcing her favorite brother-in-law and that she was finally willing to accept my partner and our relationship. I had feared a loud, ugly argument with her for bringing my partner to our family's Christmas, but was unprepared for this: we were shunned, flattened into a transparent sheet of invisibility, quarantined like some contagion to a little corner in the living room while she kept a safe, hygienic distance near the kitchen sink.

I don't know what was worse: that, or her teenage son's unabashedly gawking at my partner as if she were some animal in the zoo, objectifying her with this relentless deadening stare devoid of any semblance of humanity any time she moved or spoke—my partner, a loving, caring, supportive person whom he had never met until then. What had she ever done to him to deserve such cold and callous treatment? I just wanted to knock my sister's homophobic head against the wall and demand, "What's wrong with you? And what are you teaching your children?"

When my sister and her family finally left after what seemed like an interminably long day, it wasn't like we could scoop all that venomous animosity into a sack and toss it out with the garbage. We felt stunned and defiled long after their departure. I was angry and never wanted to see my sister or her family again.

A few days later, my partner and I began our drive home. There wasn't much traffic that weekday morning on that two-lane road in northeast Indiana. The wind cut across the stubble of soybean and cornfields, polishing the ice to a smooth, shining glaze, yet sweeping thick fingers of snow onto the pavement, fingers that grabbed at the car and tried to pull it under its thick white underbelly into the ditches. A few valiant trees keened in the face of a piercing wind and the bitter cold. Isolated farmhouses stood their ground against the sea of snow, against a sky so bright and clear it was almost painful. No sign of the usual cows or horses that were hopefully in their warm barns, munching on some oats and hay.

After about a half hour of not saying much and feeling tremendous guilt for subjecting my partner to the Christmas from hell, I glimpsed a dark figure off to the right side of the highway at a junction with a county road. This lone figure—stark against the icy whiteness and incongruent as a shout erupting from a cloistered convent—was holding up a handmade cardboard sign for the few passing motorists to read. Even driving slowly on the slick snow-covered road, I was only able to catch a few of the crayoned words: something something ... Need food.

We drove on a bit in silence but not more than a half mile when my partner and I both looked at each other. *Did you see that?* The nod: we weren't seeing things—and, unfortunately, we were. *We have to go back,* we said almost in unison. I was so relieved she felt the same way—no discussion, no argument, no brainer. I found a safe place to turn around and drove back to that county road. As we drew closer, we could make out the dark solitary figure—not a ghost, but a young woman shivering beneath the hood of her coat—and the thin scrawl on her sign: Family of 6. No heat. Need food.

And I remember experiencing this weird feeling then—a subtle interior rumbling, a shift in some deep tectonic plate within me. Because, other than forking over some spare change into the kettle of a Salvation Army bell-ringer, I have never done what I was about to do. My insides were shaking as this odd feeling was building, building until suddenly, as if some floodgate had opened, as if a dike had burst, I was scooped up in this powerful surge of giddiness, and I started rifling through my pockets and fumbling for my wallet. My partner was swept up in it too, and we threw caution to the wind, pulling out all the greenbacks we could find, all the money we had received as Christmas presents just a few days ago, easy come, easy go.

It felt like a Thelma-and-Louise breaking of the law—but for all the right reasons, as exhilarating as being plopped into the no-time-to-think torrent of the great Eastern Australian Current like Dory and Marlin in their quest for Nemo. It was skin-tingling—this unexpected shower of grace—lathering us up with a bar of zestful new life, scouring away all the dead scales of judgment and cleansing any of our recently opened wounds.

I rolled down the car window and handed the young woman our wad of uncounted cash, knowing it wouldn't go anywhere far enough to feed a family of six in a place with no heat. And with that thought, my heart shattered into a million icicles hitting the pavement, and I could barely manage to squeak out, "Take good care."

And as I resumed driving east along Highway 24 in our comfortable, adjustable heat-on-wheels, I marveled at the faith of that young woman waiting, waiting in the bitter cold of the Indiana tundra on a middle-of-the-week morning with little chance of encountering the kind of help she really needed, of not only braving the elements but also the "get a job" contempt of passing motorists, and even perhaps of her own family calling her crazy for merely thinking about going outside in that kind of weather with her flimsy plea for help.

I knew in my core that it was no coincidence that made us change our plans at the last minute, to take that two-lane instead of the tollway on that particular day at that particular time. I have come to believe that there is something that knows us better than we know ourselves, something that has our best interests at heart, giving us what we need exactly when we need it —like these little gifts of grace hidden in plain sight, huddled in a parka and standing on a snow-swept highway.

It amazes me how Spirit can raise us up out of those awful situations in our lives into ones so heartbreaking yet so uplifting, how it can transfigure feelings of woundedness and disconnection into something resplendent and glorious. I like to think of that encounter with the young woman as the Easter of our Christmas, redeeming the anguish my partner and I had endured three days prior, rolling the stone away from my dark broodings and letting in some much needed light.

About the Author

Becky Banasiak Code is a published author of numerous essays and poems. She draws inspiration from the groundedness and authenticity of nature and the great outdoors: the wildlife, valleys, hills, and mountains that invite one to discover who they really are and how they want to be in this world. She senses that she may have had some past lives as an explorer and a dog. Becky has been a regular contributor at a regional juried event called Women Speak. Her public presentations about her spiritual journey have been described by some audience members as "spiritual stand-up." She currently teaches anatomy to medical students and lives with her partner in Ohio.

www.ingramcontent.com/pod-product-compliance
Lightning Source LLC
Chambersburg PA
CBHW020539080526
44583CB00013B/913